LES MISÉRABLES

Conversion, Revolution, Redemption

TWAYNE'S MASTERWORK STUDIES

Robert Lecker, General Editor

LES MISÉRABLES

Conversion, Revolution, Redemption

Kathryn M. Grossman

TWAYNE PUBLISHERS
An Imprint of Simon & Schuster Macmillan
New York

PRENTICE HALL INTERNATIONAL
London Mexico City New Delhi Singapore Sydney Toronto

Twayne's Masterwork Studies No. 160

Les Misérables: Conversion, Revolution, Redemption
Kathryn M. Grossman

Twayne Publishers
An Imprint of Simon & Schuster Macmillan
1633 Broadway
New York, New York 10019

Library of Congress Cataloging-in-Publication Data

Grossman, Kathryn M.
    Les misérables : conversion, revolution, redemption / by Kathryn
M. Grossman.
        p.   cm.—(Twayne's masterwork studies ; no 160)
    Includes bibliographical references and index.
    ISBN 0-8057-8350-4 (cloth).—ISBN 0-8057-7832-2 (paper)
    1. Hugo, Victor, 1802–1885. Misérables.   I. Title.   II. Series.
PQ2286. G77   1996
843'.7—dc20
                                                                                    96-4191
                                                                                    CIP

The paper used in this publication meets the minimum requirements of American
National Standards for Information Sciences—Permanence of Paper for Printed Library
Materials, ANSI TK

10 9 8 7 6 5 4 3 2 1 (hc)
10 9 8 7 6 5 4 3 2 1 (pb)

Printed in the United States of America

To my parents,
Charles and Ruth Grossman

Contents

Note on the References and Acknowledgments

All page references in the text are to Lee Fahnestock and Norman MacAfee's contemporary version of Charles Wilbour's 1862 translation, first published by Signet Classic in 1987. Although there are several other English translations of *Les Misérables* currently in print, none is more faithful to the original. Still, given Hugo's poetic ear, his figurative use of language, and his fondness for wordplay, no single rendition could be completely satisfactory. I have therefore provided an alternative translation in the few cases where greater fidelity to the French was essential to my argument. I have also translated citations from all other primary and secondary sources published in French.

I would like to express my deepest appreciation to family, friends, and colleagues and, most especially, to the wonderful students at Penn State who have shared my enthusiasm for Hugo's work over the past 20 years. To John Harwood, whose critical and technical skills have served French studies so well, I am grateful for a continuing and ever-lively exchange on things Hugolian. Finally, I am indebted to the Institute for the Arts and Humanistic Studies at Penn State for supporting research for this project at the Bibliothèque Nationale in Paris.

Portrait of Victor Hugo, 1862
Félix Nadar
© 1995 Artists Rights Society (ARS), New York/SPADEM, Paris

Chronology: Victor Hugo's Life and Works

1797	Marriage of Léopold-Joseph Sigisbert Hugo, a captain in the Revolutionary army from Lorraine, and Sophie Trébuchet, an ardent royalist from Brittany.
1798	Birth of Abel Hugo.
1800	Birth of Eugène Hugo.
1802	Birth of Victor-Marie Hugo on 26 February. The number 24601 branded on the galley slave Jean Valjean in *Les Misérables* purportedly commemorates the date of Victor's conception—24 June 1801—on a peak in the Vosges mountains.
1804	Napoléon Bonaparte crowned emperor of France. Sophie moves to Paris with her three sons, effectively separating from her husband.
1807–1808	The family sojourns with Colonel Hugo in Naples, but Victor's parents fail to reconcile.
1809	Back in Paris, Sophie and her sons move into part of a former convent with a huge, untamed garden in the Impasse des Feuillantines. Here Victor is indelibly marked by the beauty, mystery, and terror of the natural world.
1811–1812	The family spends a year in Madrid with General Hugo.
1812	General Lahorie, Sophie's lover and Victor's godfather, is implicated in a royalist plot and executed.
1814	Léopold and Sophie Hugo initiate official divorce proceedings.
1815	Victor and Eugène enroll at the Cordier boarding school in Paris. The battle of Waterloo marks the end of Napoléon's empire and the restoration of the French monarchy. Victor, aged 13, starts his first notebook of verse.

1817	Begins sketching dramas in verse and prose. Receives an honorable mention in a poetry contest sponsored by the Académie Française.
1818	Eugène and Victor enroll in law school with their father's financial support, but in fact pursue literary careers. To win a bet, Victor composes his first novel, *Bug-Jargal* (*The Slave-King*), in just two weeks. The black hero, a leader of the 1791 slave uprising in Santo Domingo, prefigures the outlaw protagonist of *Les Misérables*. Eugène shows increasing signs of mental illness.
1819	Victor falls in love with his childhood friend, Adèle Foucher, a union vigorously opposed by both families. Awarded first prize for his royalist odes in a nationwide poetry contest. Founds *Le Conservateur littéraire* (*The Literary Conservative*) with his brothers and serves as its principal contributor, producing 112 critical articles in 16 months.
1820	Receives a 500-franc reward from King Louis XVIII for his ode on the death of the Duc de Berry. Publishes first version of *The Slave-King* in *Le Conservateur littéraire*.
1821	Death of Sophie Hugo.
1822	Granted a royal pension of 1,000 francs after publishing *Odes et Poésies diverses* (*Odes and Various Poems*). Marriage of Adèle and Victor, who can now afford to support a family. Eugène, who also loves Adèle, slips permanently into madness the night after the wedding.
1823	Publishes *Han d'Islande* (*Hans of Iceland* or *The Demon Dwarf*), the first French historical novel, inspired by Sir Walter Scott and set in late–seventeenth-century Norway. Joins with other aspiring young writers in founding a literary review, *La Muse française* (*The French Muse*). Birth and death of a son, Léopold-Victor.
1824	*Nouvelles Odes* (*New Odes*). Birth of a daughter, Léopoldine.
1825	Named Chevalier of the Legion of Honor. France recognizes the independence of Haiti, formerly part of Santo Domingo.
1826	Second version of *The Slave-King*. Birth of a son, Charles. *Odes et Ballades* (*Odes and Ballads*).
1827	Publishes *Cromwell*, a lengthy play destined for reading rather than the stage. Its critical *Preface* becomes the manifesto of the new French romantic movement.
1828	Death of General Hugo. Failure of Victor's first performed play, *Amy Robsart*, an adaptation of Walter Scott's novel *Kenilworth* (1821). Birth of a second son, François-Victor.

1829   Publishes *Les Orientales* (*The Orientals*), a collection of lyric poems on Eastern themes, and *Le Dernier Jour d'un condamné* (*The Last Day of a Condemned Man*), a powerful first-person narrative against capital punishment. *Marion de Lorme*, staged at the Comédie Française, is banned by King Charles X for political reasons. Hugo subsequently refuses an additional government pension of 4,000 francs.

1830   His new play *Hernani* opens to a tumultuous battle between literary conservatives and liberals, with the romantic generation claiming victory. (Verdi stages an operatic version, *Ernani*, in 1844.) In politics, too, the July Revolution sweeps away the Bourbon Restoration and establishes the constitutional monarchy of Louis-Philippe. Birth of a second daughter, Adèle (Adèle II).

1831   After eight years of marriage and five children, Adèle Hugo falls in love with Charles-Augustin Sainte-Beuve, one of Victor's closest friends, and ceases conjugal relations. Publication of *Notre-Dame de Paris: 1482* (*The Hunchback of Notre Dame*), a historical novel; and of *Les Feuilles d'automne* (*Autumn Leaves*), a collection of intimate verse.

1832   Insurrection by left-wing republicans, a forgotten historical event reconstructed in *Les Misérables* through the story of the young hero, Marius Pontmercy, and his revolutionary friends. Premiere at the Comédie Française of *Le Roi s'amuse* (*The King's Diversion*)—adapted by Verdi in 1851 for his opera *Rigoletto*—and immediate government ban for "immorality."

1833   Hugo falls in love with the actress Juliette Drouet, who will abandon her career to become his faithful companion, friend, and de facto secretary until her death 50 years later. Wins popular and critical acclaim for *Lucrèce Borgia*—the basis of Donizetti's 1834 opera, *Lucrezia Borgia*. *Marie Tudor I*, another historical drama, is far less successful.

1834   Publishes *Littérature et Philosophie mêlées* (*Literature and Philosophy Together*), a collection of critical essays; and *Claude Gueux*, a narrative indictment of the criminal justice system that foreshadows *Les Misérables*.

1835   *Angelo, tyran de Padoue* (*Angelo, Tyrant of Padua*), performed at the Comédie Française. (Ponchielli's operatic rendition, *La Gioconda*, dates from 1876.) Publishes a poetry collection, *Les Chants du crépuscule* (*Twilight Songs*), much of which echoes republican sympathies.

1836   Fails twice in his bid for election to the Académie Française. Premiere of *La Esmeralda*, an opera by Louise Bertin based on *The Hunchback of Notre Dame*.

1837	Death of Eugène Hugo at the Charenton asylum. Publication of *Les Voix intérieures* (*Inner Voices*), poetic reflections on familial and national events.
1838	Premiere of *Ruy Blas*, a play celebrating the aspirations of the lower classes and a popular triumph.
1840	Again rejected by the Académie Française. Publication of *Les Rayons et les Ombres* (*Rays and Shadows*), which contains some of Hugo's most famous lyric poems.
1841	Election to the Académie Française.
1842	Publishes *Le Rhin* (*The Rhine*), a depiction of his travels in 1839 and 1840 intertwined with history, legend, and politics. The conclusion, a historical study of the balance of power, proposes an alliance between France and Germany as a means of establishing peace in Europe.
1843	Failure of *Les Burgraves* (*The Robber Lords of the Rhine*), ending his dramatic career. Death of Léopoldine Hugo, recently married and expecting a child, and of her husband, Charles Vacquerie, in a boating accident on the Seine. Hugo is devastated when he learns the news from the paper five days later while travelling with Juliette Drouet. The event is inscribed in Jean Valjean's second brand, 9430, which can be read as "September 1843, Nothingness."
1844	Premiere of *La Esmeralda*, a ballet by Jules Perrot, based on *The Hunchback of Notre Dame*.
1845	Named Peer of France in April by King Louis-Philippe. Publicly humiliated in July after being caught in adultery with Léonie d'Aunet, the first woman to have visited the Arctic Circle on a scientific mission and wife of the painter Auguste Biard. Begins drafting a novel, first called *Jean Tréjean* and then *Les Misères*, which will become *Les Misérables*.
1847	Speech before the other peers supporting the return to France of Louis-Napoléon Bonaparte, Napoléon's politically ambitious nephew.
1848	The February Revolution interrupts Hugo's writing of *Les Misères* and inaugurates the Second Republic. Elected conservative representative to the Constituent Assembly. Begins to move Left when the government represses republican and socialist insurgents in the wake of the June riots in Paris. Founds and co-edits with his son Charles a political daily, *L'Evénement* (*The Event*), and successfully campaigns for the election of Louis-Napoléon to the presidency of the Second Republic. Speech to the Assembly against the death penalty.

Chronology

1849
Elected conservative representative to the Legislative Assembly. In his opening address as president of the international Peace Congress held in Paris, he becomes the first person on record to espouse the ideal of an "États-Unis d'Europe" (United States of Europe). His speech on poverty to the Legislative Assembly further contributes to his break with the Right.

1850
Speeches in favor of universal suffrage and freedom of the press, and against deporting political prisoners to penal colonies and allowing the clergy to control public instruction. In championing the notion of free, compulsory education, he makes the first known use of the expression *"le droit de l'enfant"* (the right of the child), a major concern in *Les Misérables* as well.

1851
Attacks Louis-Napoléon directly in speeches to the Assembly. Emprisonment of Charles and François-Victor Hugo for articles appearing in *L'Evénement* and its successor, *L'Avènement du peuple* (*The Advent of the People*), respectively. Both papers are seized and banned. Louis-Napoléon overthrows the republic. Hugo takes to the streets in a vain attempt to galvanize the working classes into resistance. After nine days in hiding, and with a price on his head, he flees in disguise to Brussels, where Juliette Drouet soon joins him with a trunkful of manuscripts. Writes *Histoire d'un crime* (*History of a Crime*), published in 1877, a scathing condemnation of the coup d'état.

1852
Napoléon le Petit (*Napoléon the Little*), a history of the period from December 1848 to April 1852 indicting Louis-Napoléon's rise to power. Exile continued in the Channel Island of Jersey. Louis-Napoléon proclaimed emperor as Napoléon III.

1853
The Hugo family participates in spiritualist séances, producing recorded contacts not only with Léopoldine, but with Isaiah, Socrates, Julius Caesar, Jesus Christ, Mohammad, Dante, Joan of Arc, Luther, Shakespeare, Rousseau, Robespierre, Byron, and Chateaubriand, among others. The séance table orders Hugo to finish his novel, which it renames *Les Misérables*. Publishes *Châtiments* (*Chastisements*), political satire and invective aimed at Napoléon III and his first poetic work to appear in the 10 years since Léopoldine's death.

1855
Expelled from Jersey, along with his sons and 32 other republican outlaws. Takes up residence in the Channel Island of Guernsey.

1856   Publishes *Les Contemplations* (*Contemplations*), subtitled "Memoirs of a Soul" and celebrated for its elegiac and visionary lyrics. Adèle II falls gravely ill, the victim of a mental disorder to which she will eventually succumb.

1859   Refuses Napoléon III's general amnesty. First series of *La Légende des siècles* (*The Legend of the Centuries*), epic poems depicting humanity's historical and spiritual progress. *La Fin de Satan* (*The End of Satan*) and *Dieu* (*God*), two related collections of visionary poetry composed in exile, are not published until 1886 and 1891, respectively. Intercedes on behalf of John Brown, the American abolitionist condemned to death for treason.

1860   Rereads the manuscript of *Les Misérables* and resumes writing where he had left off (Part 4, Book 15) in 1848.

1861   Travels to Belgium and completes *Les Misérables* at Waterloo, where he composes his famous digression on the battle (Part 2, Book 1).

1862   Publication of *Les Misérables*, first in Brussels, then in Paris. The novel achieves instant success in France and abroad.

1863   Adapted for the stage by Charles Hugo, *Les Misérables* opens in Brussels. Adèle II runs away to London, then Canada, in pursuit of an illusory romantic relationship.

1864   Hugo prefaces François-Victor's 18-volume translation of Shakespeare (1859–66) and publishes *William Shakespeare*, a meditation on artistic genius.

1865   *Les Chansons des rues et des bois* (*Songs of the Streets and the Woods*), a collection of pastoral poetry.

1866   *Les Travailleurs de la mer* (*Toilers of the Sea*), set in the Channel Islands, recounts a fisherman's heroic struggles against the forces of nature and of human passion alike.

1868   Birth of Georges, son of Charles Hugo. Death of Adèle Hugo in Brussels.

1869   Publishes *L'Homme qui rit* (*The Man Who Laughs or By Order of the King*), a novel that interweaves political, sexual, and aesthetic motifs within the historical setting of seventeenth-century England. Presides at the European Peace Conference in Lausanne. Birth of a granddaughter, Jeanne.

1870   The Franco-Prussian War brings an end to the Second Empire with the surrender of Napoléon III at Sedan. After 19 years in exile, Hugo returns to Paris the day after the Third Republic is proclaimed. He is enormously popular, having come to symbolize fidelity to the democratic ideal.

1871   Paris surrenders to the Prussians after a four-month siege. Hugo elected representative from Paris to the National Assembly but soon resigns in protest. Death of Charles Hugo. Civil war in Paris between government forces and the insurrectionary Communards; some 25,000 workers are killed in the struggle. Failed bid for reelection.

1872   Defeated again in a special legislative election. Adèle II is brought back from Barbados hopelessly demented and is institutionalized until her death in 1915. Publication of *L'Année Terrible* (*The Terrible Year*), poetry inspired by the events of 1870–71. In the face of a reactionary government, Hugo returns to his writing in Guernsey.

1873   Death of François-Victor Hugo.

1874   *Quatrevingt-treize* (*Ninety-Three*), a historical novel set during the Reign of Terror that explores the question of violence in the service of revolutionary ideals.

1875   Publishes *Actes et Paroles* (*Actions and Words*), I and II, collections of his political speeches and writings.

1876   Elected senator. Speech in favor of amnesty for the Communards. *Actes et Paroles*, III.

1877   Publishes the second series of *La Légende des siècles*, as well as *L'Art d'être grand-père* (*The Art of Being a Grandfather*), lyric poetry about the joys of family life. Plays a key role in preventing a coup d'état by President Mac-Mahon.

1878   Stage adaptation of *Les Misérables* performed in Paris at the Porte-Saint-Martin Theater. After suffering a mild stroke, Hugo ceases writing new material and contents himself henceforth with publishing previously drafted manuscripts.

1879   *La Pitié suprême* (*Supreme Pity*), a poetic work in support of amnesty. Speech on amnesty to the Senate.

1880   Publishes *Religions et Religion* (*Religions and Religion*) and *L'Ane* (*The Ass*), two long antiestablishment poems composed in exile. New attempt, this time successful, to obtain amnesty for the Communards.

1881   *Les Quatre Vents de l'esprit* (*The Four Winds of the Mind*)— satiric, dramatic, epic, and lyric verse—a microcosm of Hugo's entire poetic career. The beginning of his eightieth year is celebrated as a national festival: 600,000 Parisians pass in homage beneath his window on what is soon rebaptized "Avenue Victor Hugo."

1882	Reelected senator. *Torquemada*, a play on the architect of the Spanish Inquisition, appears.
1883	Death of Juliette Drouet. Third series of *La Légende des siècles*.
1885	Hugo dies of pulmonary congestion on 22 May. He lies in state on 31 May under the Arc of Triumph as 2 million people file past, and 1 June is declared a day of national mourning. After a seven-hour procession of delegations from throughout France and the French-speaking world (followed by several million adults and children), he is interred at the Pantheon alongside other national heroes.

LITERARY AND
HISTORICAL CONTEXT

1

Hugo's Times

The opening lines of *Les Misérables*—"In 1815 Monsieur Charles-François-Bienvenu Myriel was bishop of Digne. He was then about seventy-five and had presided over the diocese of Digne since 1806"[1]—invite us to enter Hugo's fictional universe at a pivotal moment in history: Napoléon's defeat at Waterloo in 1815. Yet the passage also points much further backward, beyond Myriel's installation in 1806 to his birth around 1740. Thus, from the outset, the book insists not only on its connection to the "real world" but on the spiral-like operation by which it continually widens its scope, encompassing ever greater chunks of "reality."

Similarly, the closing episode in the novel—the death of the outlaw hero, Jean Valjean, in 1833—is immediately relegated to the distant past by the description of his tombstone: "No name can be read there. Only many years ago, a hand wrote on it in pencil . . . four lines, which have gradually become illegible under the rain and the dust, and are probably gone by now" (1463). Once again, the temporal frame begins to shift, and the reader realizes that the interval of time indicated by the phrase "many years ago" is entirely relative and therefore indeterminate. Is the narrator, for example, speaking from the mid-1840s, when most of the text was initially drafted? From June 1848, the last period of historical significance discussed amid its many digressions? From the early 1860s, when Hugo revised and completed his manuscript? Or perhaps from some unspecified point closer to our own age, the narrator's omniscient eye surveying Jean Valjean's grave from an imagined future? The apparent chronology of the story—1815–33—is thus undercut from beginning to end by its infinitely expanding perspective. Linking the evolution of post-Revolutionary France both to the fate of earlier civilizations and to humanity's utopian destiny, Hugo reflects on and judges the present in light of past and future alike. His far-ranging text, published during exile in the Channel Islands, enables him to transcend his constricted existence through the power of the visionary imagination.

In its sweeping commentary on history from the French Revolution to the Revolution of 1848, *Les Misérables* examines the issues and events that engaged the passions first of Hugo's parents and then of the writer himself. In so doing, the novel also implicitly evaluates the aftermath of 1848, the unmentioned (and unmentionable) period preceding its publication in 1862.

Born in 1802 to a royalist mother and a republican father, Hugo experienced early on the forces of discord, the struggle for personal and political loyalties, the violence that can stem from opposing viewpoints. By the time he was one year old, his parents were no longer living together. His father, a model for the banished, unknown, and unappreciated Colonel Pontmercy in the novel's subplot, reached the rank of major in the Revolutionary army and, after Napoléon was crowned emperor in 1804, became a general in the imperial army, serving honorably in numerous campaigns and in a series of administrative posts both at home and abroad. In 1811, as the family traveled through occupied Spain to join him, ubiquitous signs of hostility and accounts of murderous guerrillas intent on driving out the French invaders revealed the depth of hatred between peoples and nations. Back again in Paris the following year, the boy's godfather General Victor Lahorie—who was also his mother's lover—was arrested at their home, where he had been hiding intermittently since 1804; he was later executed for his role in a conspiracy against the emperor. Such vivid experiences of familial and political strife are reflected in the highly dramatic quality of Hugo's fiction and in the recurrent theme of the resolution of conflict, both internal and external. In *Les Misérables*, the moral battles of Jean Valjean, a fugitive from justice who cannot escape his own conscience, closely resemble the turmoil of warfare—from the clash of armies on the plains of Waterloo to the civil uprisings of 1832—as well as the goal of achieving universal harmony.

During his lifetime (1802–85), Hugo not only bore witness to monumental changes—often accompanied by violence—in the social, political, cultural, and literary arenas. He was also an active participant in the process, sometimes striving to subvert existing institutions, sometimes helping to create new ones. With the end of the First Empire in 1814, he displayed the same exuberance for the restoration of monarchic order as the novel's young protagonist, Marius Pontmercy. Soon, other forces would come into play. Paradoxically, the stodgy regimes of Louis XVIII (1814–24) and of Charles X (1824–30), aging brothers of the king dethroned by the French Revolution and guillotined in 1793 under the Reign of Terror (1793–94), ended by stirring the imagination of a whole generation of writers. Energies that under Napoléon might have been channeled into attaining military glory were now devoted to the pursuit of literary fame and fortune. Seeking fulfillment in and through art, Hugo was terribly precocious. He began writing complete plays, echoing his fondness for popular melodrama, at the age of 14; devoured Walter Scott's historical novels as soon as each translation rolled off the press and penned his first work of fiction—whose black rebel hero foreshadows Jean Valjean—when he was 16; and composed poetry that won him national recognition, including a royal pension, before he had turned 18.

In these early ventures the young poet summarized the aspirations of many, while anticipating the broader cultural revolution about to unfold. In 1819 he founded a review, *Le Conservateur littéraire* (*The Literary Conservative*), that within two years radically shifted its critical position. Initially it espoused the orthodox, neoclassical aesthetic, which dominated the official theater of the day and forged a connection, however tenuous, between the restored Bourbon dynasty and the age of Louis XIV. But the devotee of Scott, of sensationalist drama, and, above all, of artistic freedom soon joined in backing the new (and officially reviled) school of innovators—Lamartine, Musset, Nodier, Vigny—who were labeled *romantics*. The boldness of this shift can be measured by the fact that, as late as 1830, a ferocious struggle between the two camps was reenacted night after night during the run of Hugo's first successful play, *Hernani*, over its break with dramatic conventions. At the same time, his articulate defense of the modern aesthetic, coupled with his prodigious output, had done more than designate him the leader of the romantic movement. The embrace of cultural reforms concurred with a growing intolerance, widely shared, for the erosion of civil liberties under Charles X. The lifelong enemy of repressive forces, Hugo would celebrate the fall of the Bourbon monarchy following the July Revolution, six months after the premiere of *Hernani*. The thirst for freedom of artistic expression had led the former royalist to a liberal political stance as well. Forty-one years after the French Revolution, the conservative backlash of the Restoration likewise yielded throughout France to a renewed upsurge of democratic sentiment.

Revolution did not, however, result in the reestablishment of the French Republic. Rather, as the reader of *Les Misérables* learns in the digression "A Few Pages of History" (IV.i), liberals and conservatives united to create a constitutional monarchy, thereby averting further civil disorder.[2] Under Louis-Philippe, the July Monarchy (1830–48) fostered policies that suited the prospering bourgeoisie: industrial development at home and peace with its neighbors abroad. Initial electoral reforms swelled the ranks of eligible voters. And membership in the Upper House of the French Parliament was changed from a hereditary to a lifetime peerage, effectively opening it to industrial magnates and the wealthier portion of the middle class. Yet with only 200,000 electors in a nation of 33 million (a mere 0.6%), such government remained far from representative. Social unrest assumed the form of popular demonstrations in December 1830 and February 1831, of a revolt by the Lyon silk weavers in November 1831, and—as depicted in *Les Misérables*—of the June 1832 insurrection by republican ideologues, both students and workers, on the Parisian barricades.

It would require another 16 years for full-scale revolution to occur, largely because of the country's industrial expansion, starting in late 1832 and accelerating in 1835 and well into the 1840s. Hugo's text, although set earlier in the century, also recalls the July Monarchy in underscoring the enormous benefit to a region of one successful entrepreneur—and the calamitous consequences of his downfall. For France the period of greatest prosperity, 1842–46, came to an abrupt halt when two years of poor harvests led to mass bankruptcies in the financial and industrial sectors. Starvation spread from the country to the city, from peasants to unemployed railway builders, coal miners, metalworkers, and construction crews. The face of misery and poverty was everywhere. Beginning his novel in late 1845, Hugo was able to draw on current events and personal observations to portray the wretched of the earth—*les misérables*. Moreover, like other literary figures of his day, he endeavored to effect social and political change directly, through government. Named a Peer of France in 1845 (a rank equivalent to that of a member of the House of Lords in the British Parliament), he took up over the next several years a number of causes that inform the novel as well, including prison reform, child labor laws, mercy in capital cases, and the abolition of political exile.

But for those who suffered, change was intolerably slow. Since the mid-1830s, laws limiting the freedom of the press, hard times in various sectors, and the government's continuing opposition to reform of any kind had rallied increasing numbers of workers and intellectuals to the socialist movement. In February 1848, the situation exploded into revolution, the first of many throughout Europe that year. With more than 1,500 barricades blocking the streets of Paris, Louis-Philippe was forced to abdicate and the Second Republic was immediately declared. The provisional government augmented measures to placate an armed populace: abolition of the death penalty, of slavery, of debtors' prison, of corporal punishment; restoration of freedom of the press and of the right to assembly; proclamation of the right to work and creation of labor brigades for the unemployed; reduction of the length of the official workday; universal suffrage for all men aged 21 years and older. In the June elections to the Constituent Assembly charged with forging a new constitution, Hugo himself won a seat as a conservative representative.

Within days violence again erupted, this time pitting Parisian workers against the dominant bourgeoisie, radical utopians against traditional republicans. Although the government soon triumphed, a deep and perhaps permanent chasm had opened between the Left and the Right. At least 5,000 people were killed in Paris during the June riots and their aftermath (some estimates run as high as 13,000), and 11,000 were imprisoned or deported to the French penal colonies. The author's reflections in *Les Misérables* on this and other failed revolutions—most notably the insurrection of June 1832—link discrete historical moments in a vast evolutionary scheme. As one of the temporal boundaries of the text, June 1848 clearly raises the question: what next?

The answer, known all too well to the reader of 1862, is that Napoléon's nephew, Louis-Napoléon Bonaparte, would be both the first and the last president of the fledgling republic. Hugo had vigorously supported Louis-Napoléon's return from exile after the fall of the July Monarchy, and then his presidential candidacy in December 1848, and the poet had in turn been elected a conservative representative to the new Legislative Assembly. Ironically, as the president sought to consolidate his power by courting the Right, Hugo made a definitive turn to the Left. His speeches to the Assembly championing universal suffrage, the elimination of poverty, and free, compulsory education are echoed in the novel by the narrator and the young revolutionary martyrs; the self-serving rhetoric of the ruling powers reappears in the mouths of various bourgeois, authoritarian, and/or villainous characters.

Ineligible under the constitution to run in the 1852 presidential election, Louis-Napoléon carefully allied himself with the interests of the bankers and industrialists; promoted men loyal to him to the rank of general in the French army; and used the specter of left-wing extremism to manipulate and discredit the legislative body. On 2 December 1851, he overthrew the Republic, dissolving the Assembly and calling out the army to occupy Paris. All attempts to thwart the coup d'état—including Hugo's own heroism in the streets and on the barricades as a member of the Resistance Committee—proved futile. Many republicans, the poet among them, had to flee abroad to avoid summary execution. The theme of the great outlaw, already apparent in his earliest writings, became that of Hugo's own life as well. A year later, Louis-Napoléon declared himself Emperor Napoléon III; he would remain in power until his defeat at Sedan in September 1870, during the Franco-Prussian War. Hugo never refers by name in *Les Misérables* to Louis-Napoléon or to the December coup d'état or to the Second Empire. Yet allusions abound, for example, in his reflections on Napoléon Bonaparte and on lawless uprisings and in his indictment of materialism, authoritarianism, positivism, and large-scale urban development, all of which characterized the period.

If the Second Empire brought progress and prosperity in the form of financial and industrial expansion, it did so at the price of civil liberties and enormous capital waste. Maintaining the splendor of the imperial court and engaging in war—in the Crimea, China, Italy, Vietnam, Mexico—left little to alleviate the plight of the poor. By the early 1860s Baron Haussmann had also embarked on his extensive renovation of Paris, another extravagant enterprise that rebuilt entire neighborhoods and drove up the cost of housing in the city center, forcing the working class into dismal enclaves in the outlying districts. The appearance of *Les Misérables* thus coincided with widespread misery and unrest. A worldwide economic slump in 1862 helped galvanize the reorganization of the workers' movement, which had failed so completely in 1848—the year Marx and Engels had published their *Communist Manifesto*. Now socialism was reborn in even more radical form as French workers participated in the First International, held in London in 1864. In exploring the causes and effects of social misery, *Les Misérables* was therefore very much a work of its time; in advocating the universal republic as a political ideal, it seemed to gesture toward a not-so-distant future. Despite Napoléon III's belated efforts at liberal reform, his regime would give way in a bloodless revolution to the Third Republic (1870–1940), and Victor Hugo, his implacable foe, would return home a national hero after 19 years in exile. The poet's powers of protest and prophecy would invest him with a near-legendary stature not unlike that of Jean Valjean, that other solitary outcast who in the end prevails against personal and political catastrophe.

2

Importance of the Work

During his remarkably long and productive life, Victor Hugo established himself at various moments as the most celebrated French poet, novelist, and playwright of his day. Nineteen years in political exile denouncing Napoléon III's Second Empire only added to his renown. (We might consider the parallel with the dissident Soviet writer Alexander Solzhenitsyn, who returned home in glory in May 1994 after two decades in exile.) When *Les Misérables* was published in 1862, it appeared simultaneously in Paris, London, Budapest, Brussels, Leipzig, Madrid, Milan, Naples, Rotterdam, Rio de Janeiro, St. Petersburg, and Warsaw and was translated into almost all other major languages. The novel's phenomenal success has continued ever since: it is one of the best-selling books in the world. Besides its massive dissemination as required reading in the Soviet bloc countries throughout most of this century, dozens of versions adapted for the stage, opera, cinema, and television—in French, English, Arabic, Czech, Danish, Finnish, German, Greek, Hebrew, Hungarian, Italian, Japanese, Norwegian, Portuguese, Russian, Spanish, Tamil—have reached young and old, rich and poor, readers and nonreaders alike.

Importance of the Work

What is it about this particular work that accounts for its stature as part of our international consciousness? At the most basic level, the power of *Les Misérables* derives from a gripping story well told. The adventures of the ex-convict Jean Valjean, miraculously redeemed from evil but still pursued by his archenemy, the policeman Javert, shape a plot as full of twists and turns as the treacherous labyrinths— of dark country roads, of Parisian streets and sewers, of conscience itself—that he must master in order to survive. As a modern retelling of Satan's fall from grace, the fugitive's epic struggle for moral dignity and spiritual progress taps into a wellspring of familiar images, symbols, and myths. Striving for good outside the bounds of conventional law and order, Jean Valjean is thus clearly allied with the young revolutionary heroes who fight for social justice atop the barricades. But his high purpose and martyrdom also recall other sublime outlaws, from Jesus Christ to the revolutionaries of 1789 to Napoléon Bonaparte to the exiled author himself. The use of repeating motifs to highlight the novel's moral, political, and spiritual concerns unites the plot, subplots, characters, and digressions into one tightly woven design.

In this way, Hugo confers on the secular belief in progress the full force of the myths of sin and redemption, of heaven and hell, of death and resurrection, that pervade religious thought. His focus on conflicting value systems is both enacted through a cast of memorable characters and addressed in an array of digressive remarks on historical, economic, and sociological issues. Such digressions in turn enrich the story line, heightening the reader's suspense and understanding, and hence pleasure, as events unfold. The intricate intertwining of individual development and collective endeavor, of the notions of personal and social evolution, contributes to a sense of overall harmony beyond the initially disjointed, irregular, chaotic appearance of the text.

Although the unity of Hugo's novel is primarily thematic, its structural organization is noteworthy as well. Because it does not conform to conventions of genre or composition, the text defies any attempt at classification.[1] Yet the mingling of literary styles—*le mélange des genres*—had been a hallmark of French romanticism since

11

the 1820s, with Hugo its greatest champion. Displaying in *Les Misérables* the dazzling technique of a master storyteller, the poet transcends categories by incorporating the entire range of literary genres and rhetorical registers within a single work. Elements of epic and myth are blended with dramatic and lyrical components; the grotesque is blended with the sublime, satire with romance, comedy with tragedy, realism with romanticism, observation with prophetic vision. Thus, Hugo succeeds in encompassing in one narrative all major modes of expression. The author does not so much order these ingredients as orchestrate them, so that his creation can be read as a vast verbal symphony. Through such rhetorical mastery, he places himself at the frontier of prose fiction, exploring and expanding its boundaries.

The place of *Les Misérables* in literary and social history is thus assured by a variety of factors. From the perspective of world literature, it ranks with Dante's *Divina Commedia* (1321; *Divine Comedy*), Milton's *Paradise Lost* (1667), Goethe's *Faust* (Part 1, 1808; Part 2, 1832), Proust's *À la recherche du temps perdu* (1913–27; *Remembrance of Things Past*), and Joyce's *Ulysses* (1922) as one of the most aesthetically ambitious and linguistically stunning works ever written. Within Hugo's own lengthy career, it represents both a point of arrival for his earlier works and a point of departure for those that follow. In recombining motifs from his previous drama, fiction, poetry, and polemics, the text constitutes an unusually rich imaginative universe. In aspiring to the extremes of narrative utterance, it identifies several fertile lines of inquiry to be pursued in his last three novels, composed and published over the next 12 years. Destined to inspire millions of readers but no emulators, *Les Misérables* remains in a category all its own, a creation *sui generis*. It stands, matchless, with other great works of the ages.

But the novel's significance is more than just artistic. In its own time, it challenged Hugo's readers not only to confront, through Jean Valjean, a series of wrenching moral dilemmas, but also to reexamine existing social and political conventions—thereby tacitly subverting Napoléon III's Second Empire. Today it may serve a similar purpose. As the writer proclaims in his pithy one-sentence preface:

So long as there shall exist, by reason of law and custom, a social
condemnation which, in the midst of civilization, artificially creates a hell on earth . . . ; so long as the three problems of the
century—the degradation of man by the exploitation of his labor,
the ruin of woman by starvation, and the atrophy of childhood by
physical and spiritual night—are not solved; . . . in other words,
. . . so long as ignorance and misery remain on earth, there
should be a need for books such as this. (xvii)

Stressing the connection between the text and the outside world, Hugo
implies that the concerns of the novel may be timeless. The issues that
it raises pertain to the past world—and to ours as well. After all, has
any society ever succeeded in eradicating the evils of unemployment,
sexual degradation, and child abuse? And since we obviously cannot
eliminate suffering, should we even try? Are the poor not, as the Bible
says, "with [us] always" (Mark 14.7)? That is, are they not the condition of our own prosperity, perhaps even, as the preface indicates, of
great literature? Repeatedly torn between duty and pleasure, sacrifice
and contentment, action and passivity, the hero enacts the moral struggles of "civilization" itself. In a century replete with man-made hor-
rors, *Les Misérables* continues to disturb and engage us by querying the
limits of personal and collective progress with undiminished urgency.

3

Critical Reception

The immediate, overwhelming success of *Les Misérables*, both at home and abroad, among all classes of readers, was unique in the history of printing.[1] In France, Hugo's supporters had carefully prepared the event with a massive publicity campaign. Billed as the greatest literary work of the century, the novel began appearing in serial form on 3 April 1862, when the first two (of 10) volumes went on sale. Yet the magnitude of the public's response surprised even the most committed Hugo partisans. According to reports at the time, no one had ever seen a book devoured with such fury: public reading rooms rented it by the hour; the price skyrocketed by as much as 33 percent on the very first day; by 6 April, not a single copy could be found in all of Paris (Malandain, 1071). Hugo had been paid 300,000 francs for the manuscript (the equivalent at least $1.5 million today and an astronomical price at the time) by the Belgian editor Lacroix, who made a 517,000-franc profit on his investment over the next 12 years.

While popular opinion was virtually unanimous, the many critical assessments—by about 150 reviewers in 1862 alone—fell into two major camps. Generally speaking, political, social, and religious conservatives, representing the interests of the Second Empire and the Roman Catholic Church, assailed the author's intellectual integrity, his motives, and his ambitions, as well as the perceived central message of the text. In the more vitriolic attacks, critics claimed that the passionate arguments contained in the numerous digressions merely enabled a writer paid by the page to double his earnings. The tears he shed over the wretched of this world were, they said, sold most dearly. Moreover, his ethical views were defective: to blame society for human suffering was, according to the reactionary press, to deny individual responsibility and to undermine existing institutions. In 1864, the Vatican placed *Les Misérables* on its list of forbidden books, where it remained for several years. The more progressive, republican, Protestant critics, on the other hand, defended the novel as profoundly moral. Imbued with the New Testament notions of grace, charity, and self-sacrifice, *Les Misérables* depicted the struggles of human conscience with temptation and the eventual triumph of duty over passion, of freedom over nature.[2]

But the two camps also agreed on some points. Both described the book as "monstrous," the reviewers performing a kind of "collective exorcism" in an attempt to account for its colossal success (Malandain, 1068). Whether insisting on the exoticism of *Les Misérables*, on its resemblance to Hugo's earlier fiction, on its literary predecessors from Homer on, or on other forms it might have taken, critics in effect tried to repress, dismiss, or evade the work in and of itself (Malandain, 1068–74). Sociopolitical themes appeared often in this context. Conservatives, for example, were shocked by an early scene in which the saintly bishop Myriel, a lifelong royalist, visits a former member of the Revolutionary government whose politics he abhors, and ends by asking the dying man for his blessing. The Revolutionary's vigorous defense of the Reign of Terror as the means to a better future seemed aimed at inciting a spirit of revolt, if not civil war. The novel was, in short, dangerous and, to the mind of some right-wing reviewers, should be suppressed. Liberal democrats, on the other hand, were equally disturbed by the dearth of concrete proposals for improving society. Both groups felt that politics were better left to politicians than to poets (Bach, 602–3).

By the same token, the consensus was that *Les Misérables* was hardly a literary masterpiece. With the exception of Javert, critics said, the protagonists lacked either originality or psychological verisimilitude. Fantine was modeled on Esmeralda's mother in *The Hunchback of Notre Dame* (1831). Jean Valjean was but a pale version of Balzac's villain Vautrin, and his transformation from fugitive to respected industrialist and mayor and back again was completely implausible. In his personal correspondence, Gustave Flaubert seconded these opinions when he declared Hugo's characters to be "straight as a stick, as in tragedies, . . . mannequins, little men made out of sugar" (quoted in Bach, 605).

Above all, reactionaries, moderates, and revolutionaries alike criticized the apparently chaotic composition of *Les Misérables*, its absence of order, of harmony, of structural unity. Charles Baudelaire publicly praised the work but then wrote to his mother, "This book is vile and inept," while Flaubert considered it "made for the socio-catholic riffraff, for the whole philosophico-evangelical vermin" (quoted in Bach, 608). Others who might be more favorably disposed, like the poet, novelist, art critic, and romantic comrade-in-arms of Hugo's youth, Théophile Gautier, remained silent. Charles-Augustin Sainte-Beuve, likewise an intimate friend and colleague during the early days of French romanticism, confided to his diary: "The public's taste is really sick. The success of *Les Misérables* has raged and continues to rage beyond all one might have feared. There are epidemic best-sellers."[3] In Napoléon III's neoclassical Second Empire, where formal beauty was paramount, the book was, to their taste, simply an embarrassing throwback to the romantic period. From an aesthetic as from a political standpoint, it was judged to be gravely wanting, full of serious shortcomings and pernicious tendencies (Bach, 604–8; Malandain 1074). For a century thereafter, it was ostracized from "literature" as a text "for (and adopted by) the people."[4] And yet, despite official repudiation, it continued to sell out in France and elsewhere.

In the United States, the publication of *Les Misérables* coincided with the second year of the American Civil War, marked in 1862 by the battles of Richmond, Bull Run, and Antietam and by President Lincoln's Emancipation Proclamation freeing the slaves. In a nation torn asunder, soldiers on both sides avidly read Hugo's novel, perhaps finding in his resolution of Jean Valjean's moral dilemmas and of civil conflict in France some hope for future concord, if not unity.

In England, the leading papers and periodicals reported on each new installment. As in France, the book itself was extraordinarily successful, but official reactions were mixed (some almost humorously Francophobic). An article in the *Times*—on the same page as one discussing the emancipation of the Russian serfs—bemoaned the size of the publisher's purchase price and disparaged the book's lack of verisimilitude and adversity to "the existing order of things" (26 April 1862, 7). A critic in the *Saturday Review* praised Hugo's analysis of complex, shifting feelings and "unrivalled mastery of stage effect," while lamenting his "bad taste" and repulsive theory of life (10 May 1862, 537–38; and 13 September 1862, 320). In the *Quarterly Review*, an essay extolling Hugo's powerful, transcendent use of French over "anything in the language at any period of its history" also deplored his "ignorance of social and political philosophy"; it concluded, "Not often has greater genius been placed at the service of greater nonsense" (6 July 1862, 302 and 306). The *Atheneum* portrayed the author as an "elderly acrobat" in one issue (5 July 1862, 14) and in another issue (5 April 1862, 456) deemed him "a mere pigmy as compared with M. Eugène Sue" (who had penned the melodramatic potboiler *Les Mystères de Paris* [1842–43; *The Mysteries of Paris*])." In contrast, a critic in the *Spectator* considered *Les Misérables* evidence that Hugo was the "greatest master we have alive," the "one supremely great modern dramatist" (21 June 1862, 694). The novel, the journalist marveled, was rich enough to make the reputation of six people, yet constituted but one stone in the edifice of Hugo's fame.

One explanation for such highly divergent viewpoints is the book's unprecedented heterogeneity. As critics have pointed out, *Les Misérables* is a unique work, one with no previous models that has also produced no real literary offspring or imitators (Vernier 1985, 69). A number of celebrated contemporary writers immediately grasped its brilliance and expressed genuine admiration for its moral concerns and visionary qualities. George Sand, the romantic novelist, feminist, and former republican propagandist, publicly proclaimed it a work of poetic genius. Arthur Rimbaud called it "a true poem" in his May 1871 artistic manifesto. And in 1878 Émile Zola confessed that he remained "obsessed" by the book, despite his own wholly different approach to fiction.[5] In fact, as recent scholarly investigation has shown, Zola at once denied and acknowledged his debt to Hugo by rewriting whole passages from *Les Misérables* in his own masterpiece, *Germinal* (1885), as well as in *La Fortune des Rougon* (1871; *The Fortune of the Rougons*) and *Le Ventre de Paris* (1873; *The Belly of Paris*).[6]

Among novelists abroad, Fyodor Dostoevsky devoured *Les Misérables* the year it was published; developed *Crime and Punishment* (1866) along similar lines; reread the text and used Jean Valjean as one of the models for *The Idiot* (1868–69); reread the text again in 1874; declared it superior to *Crime and Punishment* in 1877; and "continued to revere Hugo as a prophetic voice, as a modern spokesman for the idea of spiritual regeneration."[7] Likewise, *Les Misérables* was Leo Tolstoy's favorite Hugo novel and the inspiration for *War and Peace* (1865–69). While reading it in February 1863, he noted but one word in his diary—"powerful"—to characterize the experience; in a letter written in October 1891, he went so far as to assert that the book deserved to be read "in every language in the world."[8] The English poet and critic Algernon Swinburne considered *Les Misérables* the best French novel ever written and Hugo, "the greatest prose writer of his generation—in reality, 'the greatest writer whom the world has seen since Shakespeare'" (Brombert, 2).

Between Hugo's death in 1885 and the outbreak of World War I in 1914, new editions and translations of his works—including *Les Misérables*—continued to appear, some with specially commissioned illustrations. In Japan, for example, Ruïkô Kuroiwa's 1902–3 translation, entitled *Ah! Without Pity*, had a spectacular success, remaining a best-seller for at least 30 years thereafter.[9] But other, more repressive, forces were at work in France. Several major scandals in the 1890s, including the Dreyfus affair, proved horribly embarrassing to the Third Republic. As the country moved more and more to the Right, Hugo's uncompromising humanism became increasingly uncomfortable—and unwelcome. By 1902, the centenary of the poet's birth, his social and political thinking had been completely devalued. The violence unleashed on an unprecedented scale by World War I resulted in a further, artistic backlash: the horrors of modern warfare led to a period of general disfavor for the romantic movement, with its youthful idealism and artistic excesses. Between the two wars, taste ran instead to nineteenth-century "classics"—Stendhal's *Le rouge et le noir* (1830; *The Red and the Black*), Flaubert's *Madame Bovary* (1857), and Baudelaire's *Les Fleurs du mal* (1857; *The Flowers of Evil*). Hugo became the subject of quips, most notably André Gide's oft-repeated response to a 1902 survey that asked poets who was *their* poet, "Victor Hugo, alas!" and Jean Cocteau's epigram, "Victor Hugo was a madman who thought that he was Victor Hugo." Sixteen editions of *Les Misérables* had appeared in France between 1862 and 1885; none appeared between 1914 and 1933.[10]

For decades, then, it was fashionable to hold in contempt not only Hugo but also anyone who admitted liking or admiring his work. The exceptions are noteworthy. First, the communist bloc adopted *Les Misérables* as its literary Bible. Indeed, the five-millionth copy of the 1902 translation of the novel was published in November 1951 in the People's Republic of China. Modern socialists appreciated not only the hero's perpetual examination of conscience—a kind of personal autocritique—but also the theme of social progress and the underlying indictment of the bourgeoisie: in sum, the book's revolutionary implications. Other nations struggling with oppression were similarly disposed. In his autobiographical *Anti-mémoires* (1972; *Anti-Memoirs*), André Malraux recalled running into *Les Misérables* everywhere—in India, Africa, Latin America. During their 1930 meeting, Jawaharlal Nehru, a leader in India's movement for independence, told Malraux that in his country France was "the Revolution," adding that *Les Misérables* was "one of the most celebrated foreign books" there.[11] The many film versions and abridged editions for children produced throughout the first half of the century also helped keep Hugo's story alive in the popular imagination. Even "The Fugitive," a successful 1960s television series loosely based on the novel, preserved the familiar ring of the original.

Hugo's reinstatement in French "high culture" itself followed a fascinating, indirect course. Beginning in the mid-1920s, the surrealist poets André Breton and Louis Aragon claimed Hugo—the grand enemy of "good taste," opponent of traditional notions of literary psychology, and liberator of the creative imagination—as their predecessor. Other poets, including Paul Valéry, joined the chorus in 1935 to mark the 50-year commemoration of his death; meanwhile the French Left praised *Les Misérables* for embracing the proletariat's struggles against "bourgeois fascism." The Popular Front for Defense Against Fascism, founded in 1936, likewise adopted him as the model of the writer who leaves his "ivory tower" to fight alongside the people. At the same time, the far Right was again attacking Hugo's politics, denouncing not only what rightists viewed as his pacifist, humanist, egalitarian utopianism but also his identification during exile with the Old Testament prophets. As fascism marched through Europe in the 1930s, Hugo came under fire as "the most Jewish of all the great French writers" because Job, Ezekiel, Saint John the Divine, and Saint Paul were "the ancestors of the apostle of universal democracy."[12] (The anti-Semitism of this remark notwithstanding, Hugo was not Jewish.) Those who paid homage to him were reviled as traitors or idiots. One critic even denounced Hugo for preferring thieves and assassins to judges and gendarmes, revolt to common sense, Thénardier to Javert. Under the Nazi occupation (1940–44), Hugo was ideologically appropriated by both sides: the Right used his vision of a united Europe to support the historical necessity of the Franco-German alliance; the underground Resistance, which included some of the major writers of the day, used *his* resistance to the tyranny of Napoléon III as a shining example for their own struggles (Albouy, xxiv–xxxiii; Rebérioux and Agulhon, 235–36).

The turning point in the scholarly world came in the early 1950s. When President Truman's daughter visited Paris in 1951, the government displayed a Ford in her honor on what had been the pedestal of Hugo's statue, destroyed 10 years earlier by the Nazis. On the eve of the 150-year anniversary of his birth, the French communists upheld his memory against what they perceived as a crass symbol of American capitalism. In stirring rhetoric, Aragon vigorously defended Hugo as *the* French national poet, whose patriotism and global fame had put him on a par with Homer, Dante, Shakespeare, Pushkin, and Goethe.

"Hugo is the poet of the Nation . . . because of *Châtiments* [1863; *Chastisements*, a poetic excoriation of Napoléon III] and *Les Misérables*," he proclaimed. And yet, "the genius that blocked the poetic horizon long after his death . . . is even today hated like no other by all those who wilt in his immense shadow. . . . Hugo, the invincible phenomenon, he that it took a whole foreign army to lift from our public squares, [is] the most insulted poet of our history."[13] Over the next decade, attention refocused on Hugo the patriot, the advocate of social victims, the visionary of international peace—and the innovator of new modes of poetic and narrative expression.

During this period, groundbreaking studies by such French critics as Pierre Albouy, Jean-Bertrand Barrère, Léon Cellier, and Georges Poulet renewed interest in romanticism in general and Hugo in particular. The timing was excellent, since the 1962 centennial of his best-known work was fast approaching. The surge in essays on *Les Misérables* in 1962; the 1967–70 Jean Massin chronological edition of the *Oeuvres complètes* (*Complete Works*); the analyses in the late 1960s of the writer's poetic universe and of his narratives by Jean Gaudon and Richard B. Grant, respectively—all contributed to the rediscovery of France's most famous nineteenth-century author and his prose masterpiece. The shower of publications on Hugo in and around the 1985 centenary of his death completed his transfiguration from cultural outcast to literary and political exemplar. Never a centrist, he had been accepted *and* rejected by the Left *and* the Right before being recognized for his enduring centrality. The causes that he espoused in *Les Misérables* and elsewhere—the opposition to capital punishment, the rights of children and female workers, the condition of prisons, the problem of prostitution—remain some of the great social questions of the age (Rebérioux and Agulhon, 241).

As we might expect, statistics show a huge jump in sales for *Les Misérables* since 1950. Thus, of the more than 5.25 million volumes sold in France between 1950 and 1984, sales skyrocketed from around 400,000 during the 1950s to more than 2.25 million copies during the 1960s. The rate for the 1970s and early 1980s held steady at about 1.7 million per decade (Devars et al., 386). The new, popular French editions of the work published during the 1985 centenary, as well as its listing as required reading for the 1994–95 national doctoral examinations in literature, have assured a boom ever since. Sales figures for just one foreign-language edition are equally revealing. From 1982 to 1993, for example, Penguin sold 255,895 copies worldwide of its one-volume edition of Norman Denny's English translation, and by the end of 1994 the book had been reprinted 20 times. Yet the numbers are deceiving. In fact, during the first half of this 12-year period, sales totaled 85,935 volumes, or an average of 14,323 per year. In the second half, however, sales doubled to 169,960 volumes, or an average of 28,327 per year, following the spread of the London stage adaptation to the United States, Canada, Australia, and beyond.[14] Such evidence strongly suggests that Hugo's novel, so popular in its day, continues to be widely read by scholars and nonspecialists alike.

The earliest critical responses to Les Misérables had already identified some of the issues that continue to interest scholars: the novel's affinity with previous works by Hugo and others, its ideological position, the psychology of its characters, its "chaotic" structure and rejection of realism. At the same time, the text has been illuminated by a wealth of fresh approaches. Its epic, mythic, and prophetic aspects have been explored and interrelated (Albouy, Brombert, Gaudon, Grant, Simaïka). Psychoanalytic readings (Baudouin, Mauron, Richard, Ubersfeld) have disclosed a number of repeating motifs—a "brother complex," generational conflict and identification, and opposing characters who turn out to be inverse images of each other, among others—that reflect elements of Hugo's personal history. Marxist interpretations (Rosa, Vernier) have enriched our understanding of his revolutionary vision and radical utopianism, while feminist criticism (Savy) has also helped dispel the conventional view of Hugo as the grand old man of bourgeois paternalism. In a world still plagued by poverty, despair, corruption, and indifference, scholars have at last joined with general readers in appreciating not only the beauty and power but also the profound pertinence of his book to our own place and time.

A READING

4

Romance and the Sublime Outlaw

Despite its monumental length, *Les Misérables* remains one of the most approachable works of world literature. Readers who might at first be intimidated by the sheer size of the book soon find themselves turning the pages at a furious clip to see what happens next to its outlaw protagonist, Jean Valjean, and to a host of other sympathetic characters. The organization of the novel gives several clues about how to approach it. First, we notice that it is divided into five "Parts"— "Fantine," "Cosette," "Marius," "[Epic of the Rue] Saint-Denis and Idyll of the Rue Plumet," and "Jean Valjean"—four of which are named after individual characters. In this way, the text beckons us into a world of lived experiences with which we will be able to identify. Its further subdivision into 48 unevenly distributed "Books" (8, 8, 8, 15, and 9 per part, respectively) next calls attention to an exceptionally weighty Part 4, whose title alludes to both secluded love ("Idyll") and public heroism ("Epic") in the streets of Paris. We might therefore anticipate that Hugo's novel will somehow interlace personal and communal destinies, investing certain characters and events with a significance that at once amplifies and complements the impact of the story line itself.

Finally, when we look at the third-level subdivision of the text into "Chapters" (70, 76, 76, 76, and 67 per part, respectively), we are struck by the uniformity and regularity—indeed, the near-symmetry—of its underlying configuration. Beneath the multiple plot developments and digressive passages on a wide range of topics, structure and balance have not been forgotten. That there are as many as 365 chapters in a 1463-page volume also helps explain the rapid page-turning: the average section is, in fact, only 4 pages long. With each ending comes a new chapter title, most of which contain plays on words or ideas that offer provocative hints about the connection of the episode to the work as a whole. At the same time, the 365-chapter total, which suggests some connection with the calendar year, can hardly be fortuitous. Like the sequence of daily biblical readings in a liturgical lectionary, *Les Misérables* aspires to function as a kind of spiritual guide, as a means for reflecting on time and eternity, the secular and the sacred.

To this end, Hugo combines the literary traditions of romance and epic, of heroic quests that lead from sin to redemption, from the underworld to heaven, from life to death to rebirth. The ambitious, all-encompassing dimensions of *Les Misérables*, not simply in length but in imaginative and historical sweep, place it among just a handful of genuine prose epics. (Although critics concur in citing the Bible and, for instance, the thirteenth-century Icelandic *Prose Edda* in this category, there is far less consensus regarding modern texts, which might include Tolstoy's *War and Peace* [1865–69], George Eliot's *Middlemarch* [1871–72], and Joyce's *Ulysses* [1922]). Moreover, the distinctly poetic qualities of *Les Misérables*, examined in chapter 8, reveal Hugo's deeper aim: to create a contemporary work of fiction that rivals such great national verse epics as Homer's *Iliad* and *Odyssey* (ca. 850 B.C.), Virgil's *Aeneid* (19 B.C.), and Milton's *Paradise Lost* (1667). It is no coincidence that, during the interrupion from 1848 to 1860 in composing his novel, Hugo published a major collection of epic poems, *La Légende des siècles* (1859; *The Legend of the Centuries*), on the subject of human progress through the ages.

Besides displaying an encyclopedic range of theme, epic narratives—whether in poetry or prose—typically celebrate valiant individuals whose luminous exploits hold immense collective significance. In this perspective, Jean Valjean's larger-than-life character, physical prowess, and mighty moral deeds endow him with the virtues of a true epic hero. His spiritual itinerary, which follows the quest pattern of romance, assumes biblical proportions in its resemblance to both Satan's fall from grace and Christ's suffering, death, and resurrection. The many echoes between the outcast's persistent striving for perfection, the notion of Satan obtaining God's pardon in the visionary verse of *La Fin de Satan* (1854–60; *The End of Satan*), and the more lyrical account of one person's spiritual progress in *Les Contemplations* (1856; *Contemplations*) confirms the remarkable overlap between the novel and the poetic works produced by Hugo during this period.[1]

Since it is Jean Valjean's tale that ties the text together, keeping the reader in suspense right up to the end, we must carefully examine his evolution in relation to the other main characters in the story line: the good bishop of Digne, Myriel; the unwed mother, Fantine, and her daughter, Cosette; the villainous Thénardiers; the dogged police inspector, Javert; and the young hero, Marius. Of particular interest is the contribution that each of the three characters highlighted by the titles of Parts 1–3 ("Fantine," "Cosette," "Marius") makes to his moral and spiritual growth. All three, along with Myriel, are in one way or another present in the closing scene as well—a surprising conjunction, perhaps, given the huge overall cast and the large number of casualties along the way.

This reunion of several generations—deceased as well as living—around the ex-convict's deathbed nonetheless repeats one of the author's master narrative structures. As in Hugo's other fiction, the plot of *Les Misérables* emerges from and focuses on the relations of parents and children, both natural and adoptive. Thus, in *The Hunchback of Notre Dame* (1831), an archdeacon rears the deformed bell-ringer Quasimodo, who then competes with him for the affections of the Gypsy dancer Esmeralda; printing overthrows its "parent" art form, Gothic architecture; and history has its first inklings of the people deposing the king, the national father figure.[2] A later work, *Ninety-Three* (1874), explores the tensions and harmonies between an idealist revolutionary leader, his royalist great-uncle, and the uncompromising republican priest who had nurtured him into manhood; meanwhile a mother struggles against all odds to locate her three lost children, whom the Revolutionary army has taken into protective custody.

Similar patterns proliferate throughout *Les Misérables*, only on an even greater scale. Myriel converts Jean Valjean and becomes his spiritual father. Cosette is boarded with the Thénardiers, who play evil stepparents to her Cinderella before the convict rescues her and raises her as his own. Marius is brought up by his royalist grandfather, M. Gillenormand, only to discover and "adopt" the political perspective of his veteran father, Colonel Pontmercy, after the father's death. The Thénardiers rent their two youngest boys to a woman of ill repute, who passes them off to Gillenormand as his offspring in order to collect some handsome child support. The third Thénardier son, Gavroche, briefly assumes parental responsibility for the two little children, unaware that they are his own brothers. Marius's insurgent friends claim the Revolution of 1789 as their "father" and the Republic as their "mother." And Jean Valjean may or may not succeed in bequeathing his extraordinary moral valor to the next generation.

To reach this point of sanctity, the outlaw hero has pursued an adventurous course from highly unpromising beginnings, a course that touches on and is touched by the lives of many others. The first is Myriel. Released from prison after serving a lengthy, unjust sentence, Jean Valjean is a ticking time bomb when he arrives on the bishop's doorstep in Digne. Progressive hatred—of the law, of society, of the human race, of creation—has primed him to lash out in random vengeance; his soul has "withered" (93) and all but died. To his amazement, Myriel welcomes him warmly; shares his dinner, home, and hearth; calls him "brother" (76); and urges him to replace anger with "goodwill, gentleness, and peace" (77) in order to be worthy of respect. He must leave prison behind in heart as well as body. Yet the good priest's words and deeds have little effect, for Jean Valjean robs him as he sleeps. Only a vision of Myriel's "luminous . . . conscience" (101) deflects the intruder from his murderous intentions.

What saves him is not Myriel's initial kindness and generosity but the revelation of a different moral order altogether. The scene is riveting and unforgettable. When the police arrest Jean Valjean, the bishop obtains his release by affirming that the silver had been a present: "Do not forget, ever, that you have promised me to use this silver to become an honest man," he declares. " . . . [Y]ou no longer belong to evil, but to good. It is your soul I am buying for you. I withdraw it from dark thoughts and from the spirit of perdition, and I give it to God!" (106). Myriel not only lies to the authorities; he stakes an extraordinary claim to Jean Valjean's soul through a promise that had, in fact, never been made. In an inversion of Faust's bargain with Satan, he purchases a soul from evil and dedicates it to the forces of good. The mental and emotional chains that keep the former galley slave shackled to his past have been broken. Rather than punish Jean Valjean for stealing, as the culprit himself had anticipated, Myriel rewards him with the greatest possible good. As in the Christian concept of salvation, the priest not merely buys (*achète*) his soul; he redeems (*rachète*), recovers, buys it back, through self-denial. And Jean Valjean can repay him for this wondrous gift, not just of the silver but of freedom and life itself, in only one way: by becoming another person. Having violated Myriel's hospitality and trust, he no longer has a choice about existing henceforth in "goodwill, gentleness, and peace." He must do so in acknowledgment of the bishops's sacrifice, confidence, and esteem. Through this unmerited act of grace, everything suddenly shifts from the past to the future, from his terrible, undeserved sufferings to the expectation that he will become an inexhaustible fountain of love.

Impossible as such a change might seem, Myriel has already provided Jean Valjean with the necessary example. First, he has created a new causal sequence by rendering good for evil. He has replaced the vicious circle of crime, punishment, and revenge with an open-hearted, open-ended gesture. He has also succeeded in turning one of his inventions into reality—the untruth about having given away his silver—by donating it belatedly to the thief. To fulfill Myriel's other fiction about the nonexistent promise, Jean Valjean need only keep the pledge in retrospect. His conversion thus begins as a transformation of perspective, when he apprehends the peculiar logic of love and forgiveness. If the ex-convict had asked for the silver, Myriel would have offered it without hesitation. So he donates it after the fact instead. Likewise, if Jean Valjean had been able to commit himself to starting anew, he would have done so of his own accord before. Still, it is not too late to conduct himself from now on as if the promise had really been made. In other words, his future actions are all that count. The past is dead and gone, blocked off by Myriel's divine intervention in his life.

The full meaning of the saintly bishop's challenge does not, however, dawn on Jean Valjean all at once. It takes a second crime, even more odious—stealing money from a child—to complete his conversion. The little boy, Petit Gervais, is a chimney sweep: he is most likely parentless, impoverished, and doomed to die young. When Jean Valjean realizes how low he has sunk, what terror and distress he has caused an innocent creature, with what meanness and ingratitude he has responded to another's magnanimity, he is seized by the "invisible power" (110) of his bad conscience. Falling to the ground he cries, "I'm such a miserable man!" (110; *Je suis un misérable*"), a moment of self-awareness that expresses his sense of both wretchedness and villainy. He sees himself no longer as a victim of society, but as the lowest kind of scoundrel.

One insight leads to others. His soul, he finds, is at stake in an immense internal battle: "the struggle, a gigantic and decisive struggle, had begun between his own wrongs and the goodness of [the bishop]" (111). This inner epic—which forecasts his moral quandaries in "A Tempest Within a Brain" (I.vii.3), "The Blotter Talks" (IV.xv.1), and "Immortal Jecur" (V.vi.4)—pits Jean Valjean's dark personality against Myriel's splendor in a remarkable extended metaphor. The sun that rises on and illuminates his conscience, showing him as he really is, is the good priest himself. The experience is dazzling: "as his reverie continued, the bishop grew larger and more resplendent to his eyes; Jean Valjean shrank and faded away. . . . Suddenly he disappeared. The bishop alone remained. He filled the whole soul of this miserable man with a magnificent radiance" (113). Jean Valjean's sense of self wanes completely, eclipsed by Myriel's moral superiority. In being, as it were, swallowed up by his opposite, he is able to identify with the bishop, to incorporate him as the voice of conscience. As a result, the ex-convict can judge himself objectively for the very first time. His entire existence passes before his eyes, "but in a light he had never seen before. He could see his life, and it seemed horrible; his soul, and it seemed frightful. There was, however, a gentler light shining on that life and soul. It seemed to him that he was looking at Satan by the light of Paradise" (113). As a social reprobate flung, like Satan/Lucifer, into outer darkness (Grant, 158), Jean Valjean recognizes his fallen nature and, at the same time, the possibility of redemption. The two intuitions are complementary. In accepting who and what he is, he can at last free himself from his prison of hate, the most horrible prison of all.

With the hero's conversion apparently assured, the reader is left in suspense about his next move while the narrator introduces Fantine, the titular character of Part 1. The book seems to be starting all over again—for the third time, one could say—in another city, in another year, with another cast. By the time we rejoin Jean Valjean some six years later, now a wealthy industrialist and the mayor of Montreuil-sur-mer living under the assumed named of M. Madeleine, we have encountered yet a fourth "beginning." On the one hand, such abrupt narrative leaps underscore the galley slave's ability to break with the past, to make fresh starts, to be ever alert and agile—an ability that serves him well throughout the rest of the novel. On the other, they direct our attention to the qualities of other characters and issues that Hugo will intertwine with the central plot. Fantine's short and tragic story is so often neglected in the critical literature that one might think it inconsequential. But given the title of Part 1, it is clear that she plays a key role. Her innocent, carefree "beginning," well before she reaches Montreuil-sur-mer, thus contrasts sharply with what ensues and enriches Hugo's portrayal of the ways in which nineteenth-century society victimizes women.

Again, the spectacular events of the Champmathieu affair, which redirect M. Madeleine/Jean Valjean's destiny, tend to dominate a first reading of *Les Misérables* and so to overshadow Fantine's own martyrdom and legacy. In a second reading, since we already know what happens, we can better appreciate the subtler episodes. To understand Fantine's relation to Jean Valjean, let us take a closer look at the affiliation between Jean Valjean and Champmathieu. It is evident, for instance, that the poor wretch who is accused of being the escaped parolee and who risks being imprisoned for life in his place is, in more ways than one, the hero's double. Madeleine's moral dilemma reaches epic magnitude when he must choose between saving Champmathieu and preserving the community whose prosperity depends on him: "To write the poem of the human conscience, if only of one man, even the most insignificant man, would be to swallow up all epics in a superior and definitive epic. The conscience is the chaos of chimeras, lusts, and temptations, the furnace of dreams, the cave of the ideas that shame us; it is the pandemonium of sophisms, the battlefield of the passions" (220). His dramatic conversion was not completed in a single flash of light, but must be continually reaffirmed and renewed.[3] Yet examining one's conscience can lead to conflict as violent and terrifying, the narrator asserts, as the colossal struggles depicted in Homer, Dante, and Milton. In internal, psychological warfare, one can be almost literally of two minds.

In this case, the interior monologue is actually a dialogue between two identities that each lay claim to the same man. To attain inner peace requires the harmonizing of these clashing voices. Madeleine considers the old Valjean dead and buried; the rescue of a single person is secondary to the survival of the many. To achieve the greatest good for the greatest number, the mayor thinks that the hapless Champmathieu would make a wonderful "substitute" (224) for his own alter ego. With "Jean Valjean" recaptured, tried, and sentenced, he could be "present [in prison] in the person of this Champmathieu, present in society under the name of M. Madeleine" (224). But another voice, that of Jean Valjean himself, demands that the fugitive be publicly resurrected in order to satisfy the highest laws of conscience. The other self that must be sacrificed is not Champmathieu but Madeleine, who must denounce himself at the upcoming trial: "So he had to go to Arras, save the false Jean Valjean, turn in the true one" (227). Jean Valjean can remain pure in the eyes of the bishop only by being reviled by society. Champmathieu may be a miserable, ill-fated dullard; his wretchedness makes him all the more worth saving. Indeed, the less Champmathieu resembles Madeleine, the more he resembles the convict before his conversion. Just as Myriel had shown mercy to the basest of creatures, so he must deliver this man—*his* "brother"—from unnecessary suffering.[4]

The question of identity and identification at stake in this crisis elucidates the hero's rapport with other characters, including Fantine. Jean Valjean actually speaks very little in the course of the novel. We are left to judge many of his actions by what others say about him or by what he has said or thought in other circumstances. The Champmathieu affair thus offers a mine of invaluable information through Madeleine's protracted internal debate in "A Tempest Within a Brain" (I.vii.3), as well as through the indirect discourse that reveals his state of mind at the trial itself. When the smoke clears from the psychological battle, the victor who emerges is a transfigured Jean Valjean. He is no longer a rejected, forgotten, subsidiary identity for Madeleine, with no more reality than Champmathieu. Rather, it is Madeleine who does not exist and whose rise to prominence and respectability must therefore be deemed a false route to redemption. The mayor insists that he is *not* Jean Valjean, nor does he have any responsibility for the fugitive's unlucky look-alike. Jean Valjean inverts this false logic by realizing that he *is* Madeleine, a man capable of great good, but that he could easily have become a Champmathieu—or worse—instead.

When he first picks out the accused in the courtroom, he "thought he was seeing himself" (265), an older version of how he looked on the day he entered Digne. Then he notices that the whole scene effectively recreates his own trial: "It was all there—the same paraphernalia, the same time of night—almost the same faces, judge and assistant judges, soldiers and spectators" (266). Like Jean Valjean, Champmathieu will be the victim of a miscarriage of justice, unless someone intervenes to help him. The sense of identification is so strong that, for the hero, it was not just his mirror image but "another self that faced him" (266). The timeless setting, the presence of the crucifix, the agony of accused and savior alike—all point to the martyrdom of *les misérables* in general and to Jean Valjean's Christ-like compassion and self-sacrifice in particular (Grant, 160). The path to salvation does not lead upward through Madeleine's assumed life; it requires another fall, a symbolic death by returning to prison, yet again a fresh start.

Fantine's role in fostering the outlaw's spiritual progress is equally important, though less obvious. For, even before learning of Champmathieu's case and committing himself to a course of action, Madeleine was involved in the troubles he had caused someone else. Champmathieu faces a life sentence because he looks and behaves like Jean Valjean. Javert arrests Fantine for assaulting a passerby, after she has lost her job in Madeleine's factory and turned to prostitution to support herself and her child. As the policeman goes on, "conducting a trial[,] . . . trying and condemning" (191) the terrified woman, the mayor breaks in and demands her release. The symmetry of the two cases indicates that Fantine, too, enters into a system of alternative selves with whom Jean Valjean can identify. Her pathetic speech to Javert, foreshadowing Champmathieu's disjointed address to the court, demonstrates both the devastating effects of ignorance and illiteracy and the necessity of speaking for those who cannot speak for themselves. Madeleine, who had seen the original incident, exonerates Fantine; Jean Valjean exculpates Champmathieu; Hugo takes the floor on behalf of the silent, victimized masses.

Yet Madeleine winds up interesting himself in Fantine for reasons that surpass the circumstances of her arrest. When she spits in his face—another illegal act, but this time one that will require personal forgiveness—he has the first hint that his entrepreneurial career might turn out to be a spiritual dead end. On hearing her story, he finds himself implicated in tribulations at least as horrendous as his own or Champmathieu's. Because of the stringent rules of his workshop and his delegation of authority, she has gone from the joy of "earning her living" (177) honestly to selling her body just to keep Cosette alive. Madeleine had only initiated the sequence of events by directing that the women employed at his factory have "good morals" (160). Jealousy, gossip, and bigotry had collaborated to uncover the secret of her child, which the overseer had then used to fire her.

Of all this, the mayor had known nothing. But his reaction to her tale speaks volumes: "I will pay your debts, I will have your child come to you, or you will go to her. You shall live here, in Paris, or wherever you wish. I take charge of your child and you. You will not have to work anymore, if you do not want to. . . . You will become honest in again becoming happy. More than that, . . . I declare to you from this moment . . . that you have never ceased to be virtuous and holy before God. Poor woman!" (199). The impersonal system will give way to lavish care for the martyred mother. If this seems to be an over-reaction on Madeleine's part, his exclamation at the end suggests the shock of recognizing his own responsibility for her suffering. While he was sneaking around town leaving money for the poor and otherwise doing good in secret, a woman unable to keep her job had been reduced to utter physical and social degradation. She has endured hor-rors—as both a woman and a mother—of which he had never even dreamed. His paternalistic organization, intended to protect female workers from temptation and dishonor, had had the opposite effect. Once fired, she lacked the education, skills, and prospects to support two people. Now Madeleine wants to right the wrongs and restore Fantine's happiness and dignity.

At first, the text suggests, he wants to redeem her, to buy her back from misery, by paying her debts and future expenses in a care-free new life with Cosette. He would liberate her from hatred as well as misery, much as Myriel had freed him years before. But there is, finally, "[m]ore than that" (199) in Fantine's situation. Jean Valjean can identify with Champmathieu because the poor man's existence corresponds in so many ways to his own, and because he knows all too well what prison life will do to him. Fantine, however, has borne adversity not for her own sake but for another's. In other words, she has made sacrifices for Cosette that outstrip anything that Madeleine is prepared to do on their behalf. Her limitless devotion to her child's welfare has already redeemed her, he realizes, "before God" (199). Her body may be defiled; her soul is "virtuous and holy" (199), a stun-ning example of dedication that he is bound to follow hereafter. She is, he thinks, a "martyr here below," one whose self-immolation reminds him of the "martyr on high" (200). This notion also recurs years later: when Cosette wonders if her mother was "close to sanctity in her life," Jean Valjean responds, "Through martyrdom" (891). Fantine is not just someone who, like Champmathieu, needs to be saved. Along with

Myriel, she provides a model of self-abnegation that steers the ex-convict toward the right moral track. One might even say that, from a certain point of view, *she* rescues *him*. In showing what spiritual heights can be reached by those who, in the eyes of the world, fall most low, she prepares Madeleine for the showdown in Arras and for his return to prison as Jean Valjean.

The great complicating factor, of course, is that in vindicating Champmathieu, Madeleine will be unable to keep his promises to Fantine. He has no idea that he is about to embark on a similar journey when he tells her, "This hell you have just left is the first step toward Heaven. You had to begin there" (201). The mayor's "hell" entails falling from bourgeois "grace" and reentering the penal system as a galley slave, but only in part. As his mental "tempest" evinces, it consists, too, in abandoning his community of workers. No longer free to do as he pleases, he takes the road to Arras rather than to Montfermeil, delivering Champmathieu in place of Cosette. His civil standing vanishes, and with it his legal authority. Javert can refuse him permission to bring Fantine her child before making an official arrest. Even worse, the policeman can hasten her death by stripping away all her hopes and illusions.

Although Jean Valjean is powerless to rehabilitate Fantine or to reunite her with Cosette or to prevent the economic ruin of Montreuil-sur-mer and the surrounding region, his escape from the prison ship in Toulon permits him to begin making amends for all these shortcomings. First, he saves the life of another convict, the initial installment on his debt to the general human community. Symbolically plunging into the harbor afterward, he reiterates the theme of falling in order to rise. Then, he liberates Cosette from her bondage to the Thénardiers and raises her as his own daughter. The reader is not privy to the words that Madeleine whispers into the ear of the dead mother. At the least, he tackles the one portion of the original vow that he can possibly fulfill: to "take charge of [her] child" (199). We can also imagine that he promises to make up to Cosette for all that Fantine had suffered. A pledge of this nature would clarify the deathbed scene, where Jean Valjean at last discloses to Cosette the name of her mother and adds, "She suffered a great deal. And loved you very much. Her measure of unhappiness was as full as yours of happiness. Such are the distributions of God" (1461). After intervening in Champmathieu's downward spiral, Jean Valjean miraculously appears in order to lift a little girl's burden in the Montfermeil woods, to sustain and nurture her in heart, mind, body, and soul, whatever the cost, for the rest of his life.

The ex-convict's fabulous strength and superhuman deeds so dominate the action in *Les Misérables* that it is easy to miss another, contrary pattern of imagery that defines him as well. What Fantine bequeaths to Hugo's virile hero is not just Cosette or parenthood, but maternity itself. The transfer takes place immediately after her death, when Jean Valjean arranges her head on the pillow, "as a mother would have done for her child" (294). Nine months later, having rescued Cosette on Christmas Day, he "felt his heart move again"; and so, he watches her sleep with delight, aware of "inward yearnings, like a mother" (436; *sentit se remuer ses entrailles . . . des épreintes comme une mère*). A more literal translation of this passage—that he experiences "a stirring in his entrails" and "straining like a mother [in childbirth]"—reveals the extent to which Jean Valjean identifies with Fantine. She lives on in him, as does Myriel, enabling him to love for the very first time one particular person, affectionately, thoroughly, inexhaustibly. Through him, Fantine's dreams come true. "My daughter will play in the garden. . . . I'll teach her to spell. She'll run on the grass chasing butterflies, and I'll watch her. Then there'll be her first communion" (287), she muses just before her death. Jean Valjean subsequently teaches Cosette to read; watches her at play in the convent garden; sees to her religious and secular education; and eventually moves into a house with a large, wild garden where she can chase butterflies. Cosette comes to consider him as the essence of the absent, unknown parent. As the narrator explains, "she imagined that her mother's soul had passed into this good man and come to live with her" (890). Sometimes she goes so far as to say to herself, "This is perhaps my mother, this man!" (890). The repetition of the motif signals that Cosette is not reflecting on Jean Valjean's maternal care and concern alone. Rather, she is aware that, on the day she met him, she was reborn to life.

But Cosette gives as much as she receives. Imagery of rebirth, we have seen, accompanies Jean Valjean's conversion, the disinterment of his real identity in the Champmathieu affair, and his "resurfacing" after an apparent death at sea. In assuming responsibility for a child's welfare, he undergoes further renewal. Recent insights into human wickedness and social misery—Javert's narrow-minded embodiment of public authority, the dreadful "lot of woman summed up in Fantine" (439), his imprisonment for honorable behavior—have at moments embittered and disgusted him. He needs a "fresh supply of goodness" to maintain his spiritual momentum: "Who can tell whether Jean Valjean was on the verge of discouragement and falling back on evil ways? He loved, and he grew strong again. Alas, he was as frail as Cosette. He protected her, and she gave him strength. Thanks to him, she could walk upright in life; thanks to her, he could persist in virtue. He was this child's support, and she was his prop and staff" (439). For the first time in his existence, he needs someone else. Their symbiotic relationship, in which each upholds the other, accounts for the extent of his loss at the end. She becomes his "light, family, homeland, paradise" (1154), replacing the entire community he had forfeited at Montreuil-sur-mer. It is difficult to ignore the semi-incestuous nuances of "The Blotter Talks" (IV.xv.1), where his affection is explicitly compared to that of a father, mother, grandfather, son, brother, and lover all rolled into one. Hugo's own grief over the drowning of his oldest and closest child, Léopoldine, soon after her marriage in 1843, is transparent. But we may also read Jean Valjean's multifaceted attachment to Cosette metaphorically, as a way of saying that she is the whole world to him, and that through her he loves the whole world.

Because her name is conferred on Part 2 of Les Misérables, Cosette takes on a special significance both in the outlaw's life and in the novel itself. Because of her, Jean Valjean allows himself to be buried alive in the Vaugirard cemetery as a means of securing their permanent entry into the convent. He is thus "resurrected" to two new experiences: parenthood and monastic existence. Five years in the Petit-Picpus convent cure him of any lingering revulsion at human frailties. Though he feels that he can never measure up to Myriel, he has recently been tempted by pride in comparing himself with the rest of humanity. He now finds himself in a place, like prison, full of inmates, but inmates who devote themselves to "forgiving men their sins and expiating them in their stead" (571). The nuns resemble Fantine in their sublime self-denial; they deepen the mystery by their innocence and chastity. Since Hugo was by no means a supporter of organized religion—which he considered one of the more reactionary forces of his day—the chapters on monastic life must be viewed in the context of broader concerns. With Myriel, Fantine, and the revolutionaries who defend the barricades (another kind of "prison"), the men and women who sacrifice themselves for others must be valued in and of themselves. They must be remembered when experience breeds cynicism—a form, we are told, of egotism.

So it is with Jean Valjean, who takes the harder route of leaving the convent later on, when Cosette is 14, to keep from "appropriating and plundering" (879) her happiness in order to preserve his own. The convict in a sense relives his encounter with Petit Gervais and gets it right this time: it is wrong to steal from a child. The agony of the blotter scene, after he discovers Cosette's love for Marius, repeats the pattern. He can either assist in her passage to another existence, independent of his, or he can fight to keep her for himself. The automatic response is self-centered: "Down to the roots of his hair he felt the immense awakening of selfishness, and the self howled in the abyss of his soul" (1154). But then conscience—that other, higher sense of self—takes command. For Cosette's sake, Jean Valjean relinquishes all claim to earthly happiness. He saves Marius's life, assures her fortune, denounces himself as a convict, and exiles himself from the young couple's home. Giving up everything that he cares about, even the pleasure of simply seeing his child, he fulfills his destiny as a Christ figure who feeds others on his own substance.

By the same token, Cosette enjoys a more emblematic role as well. Just as Fantine can be a well-defined individual, epitomize selfless devotion, and represent the "lot of woman" (439) all at once, Jean Valjean's adopted daughter functions on several textual levels. A father of four who had immortalized his children in verse, Hugo distills in Cosette his reflections on offspring in general.[5] As a composite character, she replaces the galley slave's whole original family of seven little nieces and nephews. She also casts a new perspective on past, present, and future. In caring for Cosette, Jean Valjean can redeem his crime against Petit Gervais and his responsibility for Fantine's ruin. She saves him from bitterness after his return to prison, filling his existence with playfulness and cheer. And she opens a window for him into tomorrow: not only does she enable him to pass on his wisdom and learning; she forces him to weigh the long-term effects on *her* of *his* current actions. From an abused child with little hope and no future, she blossoms into a kindhearted, educated, well-mannered young woman.

Some may read her as a flawed character. Certainly, by late-twentieth-century standards, the teenage Cosette seems vapid, frivolous, and oversubmissive in her relations with both Jean Valjean and Marius.[6] Lest our judgment be too harsh, however, we should remember the social context. French girls in the 1820s could receive instruction at home or in a convent, the latter entailing the equivalent of a solid elementary education. At the time of her marriage, Cosette is only 17 or 18 and still has much to learn. But her very innocence and carefree existence are what Jean Valjean had most wanted to restore to the Thénardiers' child-slave. When we consider the antithetical course of Eponine, born in the same year as Cosette and, in the end, her miserable double, we can more easily understand and accept this portrait of a little girl who grows up lighthearted and happy. Jean Valjean's investment in her, like Myriel's in him, points to the inherent worth and untapped potential of all children, a theme explored elsewhere as well. Neither heredity nor environment can, in the novel's system, fully account for or limit the human spirit. The many generous actions of Gavroche and Eponine, for instance, despite their criminal parentage and wretched conditions, highlight the need to rescue far more youngsters from social blight. When Jean Valjean fades away, making room for the next generation, he is not just ensuring that Marius and Cosette's life will be free of scandal or providing Hugo with a dénouement. He is exemplifying an attitude of humility and respect toward the new bearers of humanity's future.

In chapter 8, we will probe the structural parallels between Marius and Jean Valjean, between younger and older protagonists. Yet the story line depends in large measure on their opposition and rivalry for Cosette's love. In doing all that he can for the child he loves, the convict meets the challenge of risking his life for the young man he hates. The self that "howl[s] in the abyss of his soul" when it is clear that Cosette has been wooed and won awakens "a specter, Hatred" (1155). Threatening to undo all of Jean Valjean's moral progress since his initial conversion, the crisis leads him simultaneously to the highest and lowest points of his quest for redemption and inner harmony. The "idyllic" trysts of the lovers in Cosette's garden are matched by his "epic" conflicts within—conflicts mirrored by events on the revolutionary barricade. The hero follows Marius into the storm, but to what end? We are never told whether he plans to save the youth, eliminate the competition, or commit suicide by dying with the defenders of a hopeless political cause. As in the Champmathieu affair, the resolution of warring voices occurs not through a conscious decision reported by the narrator, much less by Jean Valjean's soliloquy, but by actions that speak for themselves.

Hugo's sublime outlaw does not enter the barricade violently. Instead, he drops his National Guard uniform, "as if from heaven" (1187), in a providential gesture that will enable a fifth insurgent to escape alive. Thereafter, he does everything in his power to protect revolutionaries and government soldiers alike. Inventive sharpshooting ends by taking no lives and sparing many. A misdirected bullet even sets Javert free, thereby contradicting the policeman's preconceived notions about his lifelong target. Jean Valjean has just one more miracle to accomplish, and then he will be ready to disappear forever into the penal system. To spring Marius from the death trap that claims all his friends is to plunge, once again, into apparent ignominy: he must descend into the Paris sewers, the gravely wounded young man on his back, and slog through miles of filth to reach safety. Years before, he remembers, he fell from the street into the convent with Cosette; now it is Marius whom he carries, not into another earthly paradise, but into the bowels of hell itself.

The narrator evokes the Dantesque dimensions of this spiritual adventure: "After the flashing whirl of the combat, the cavern of miasmas and pitfalls; after chaos, the cloaca. Jean Valjean had fallen from one circle of Hell to another" (1277). He will be lucky to escape alive; that is, with his soul intact. The nightmare scenario by which he must blindly find his way, first to Arras for Champmathieu's trial, then along the winding Parisian streets to refuge in the convent, returns with a vengeance as he stumbles through the underworld maze looking for an exit. At the same time, the text furnishes an important clue regarding the fugitive's method of navigation. Using terms like *combat, cavern,* and *chaos,* the narrator recalls the earlier depiction of the human conscience as "the chaos of chimeras, . . . the cave of the ideas that shame us . . . , the battlefield of the passions" (220). Here, then, as elsewhere, Jean Valjean retraces his internal struggle between duty and desire by attempting to traverse a labyrinth. To negotiate his own twisted feelings, he must rely on conscience, that "compass of the Unknown" (517) that enables one to see in moral darkness.

In this case, Hugo's hero descends into the sewer of his own repressed egotism in wanting to keep Cosette to himself. The "Hatred" (1155) that erupts when he reads her letter to Marius in the mirror is still present, even as he saves the young man's life. Although he handles Marius with "all the gentleness of a brother for his wounded sibling" (1290) when bandaging his wounds, he looks at him with "an inexpressible hatred" (1291). Thénardier's ethos of vengeance would justify killing his rival outright. Javert's adherence to the letter of the law would rationalize leaving the unconscious revolutionary, an enemy of the state, to die. Jean Valjean's superior conscience clings to the spirit of the law through "thought, meditation, prayer" (517) and follows its dictates wherever they may lead. He is, like the novel's felons, an outlaw (in French, *un hors-la-loi*; literally, a person outside or beyond the law), not because he fails to obey the legal code, but because his actions far surpass its expectations. In treating both total strangers and adversaries as if they were "brothers," he continues to triumph over the worst enemy of all—the evil that lurks within.

Jean Valjean's physical trial in the sewer thus corresponds to his inner, ethical ordeal. As ever, faith guides his steps in the right direction: "He went on anxiously but calmly, seeing nothing, knowing nothing, plunged into chance, that is to say, swallowed up in Providence" (1280). He has descended, Christ-like, into a modern version of hell—the city's digestive tract—his mind's eye on heaven (Grant, 170–72). Hugo's mastery of metaphoric language becomes apparent in the use of images of engulfment (*plunged, swallowed up*) to represent both falling downward and rising upward. The two are not antitheses; they are united through Jean Valjean's transcendent morality. After the temptations of "He Also Bears His Cross" (V.iii.4), the challenge reaches its climax. Reaching what may well be a bottomless pit within the sewer, the convict-saint must choose between jettisoning his heavy cross—Marius's seemingly lifeless body—and perhaps submerging in the excremental quagmire. He sinks deeper and deeper but persists in advancing until he is, so to speak, nearly ingested, still holding Marius above his own head. "In the old pictures of the deluge," the narrator notes, "there is a mother doing this with her child" (1297). At this moment, nine years after he had adopted Cosette, Jean Valjean gives new life to Marius as well, miraculously delivering him in what amounts to a gigantic (re)birth canal.

This stirring scene also encapsulates the galley slave's spiritual regeneration. Since his conversion by Myriel, his invention of a moral self has required successive leaps of faith into the unknown—where he has always encountered solid ground on the other side. He has survived "drowning" in the Toulon harbor and being buried alive in a nun's coffin—both episodes that in fact rehearse his encounter with possible asphyxiation in the sewer. In recovering his footing at the bottom of the cloaca, he thus enacts a symbolic death and resurrection: "He rose, shivering, chilled, filthy, bending beneath this dying man, whom he was dragging on, all dripping with slime, his soul filled with a strange light" (1298). By pursuing his unerring moral course, even to the foulest of depths, Jean Valjean emerges so utterly transfigured that no one recognizes him afterward. His subsequent dealings with both Thénardier and Javert, however dangerous, strike the reader as much less perilous—and so less exciting—than the joint ventures of body and soul.

By the close of *Les Misérables*, Jean Valjean's spiritual itinerary has led to triumph over love and hate, pride and despair, pleasure and pain, demonic forces both inside and outside. Whereas Javert must follow a rule book to differentiate between right and wrong, good and evil, Hugo's sublime social outcast heeds the self-imposed law of conscience alone. Throughout his career, he never loses his inner bearings, responding in everything to the voice of conscience. As he declares toward the end to Marius: "Yes! I am informed against. Yes, I am pursued! Yes, I am hunted! By whom? By myself. It is I myself who bar the way before me, and I drag myself, and I urge myself on, and I check myself, and I exert myself, and when a man holds himself in check, he is well held" (1397). The shift from the first person (*I, myself, me*) to the third person (*a man, himself, he*) dramatizes the hero's ability to project himself into everyone else, to identify empathetically with different viewpoints, to confirm his sense of self by fulfilling the needs of others. Combining Myriel's infinite compassion with Javert's implacable sense of duty, Jean Valjean has become a law unto himself—one that demands continual self-sacrifice and self-effacement. The more he loses himself through acts of devotion, the more he both affirms his own uniqueness and confirms his place in the divine scheme.

We turn now to the ex-convict's role within the wider scope of *Les Misérables*, paying particular attention to its social and political themes. After exploring the historical and satirical elements of the text in chapters 5 and 6, we will look in chapter 7 at Hugo's use of dramatic conventions to stimulate and focus the reader's attention. Finally, in chapter 8, we will examine the novel's poetic elements. The overarching theme of progress will, in the end, illuminate the multiple links between satire and prophecy, past and future, Jean Valjean and Marius.

5

Historical Perspectives

As the nucleus of *Les Misérables*, the story of Jean Valjean has dominated many abridged versions of the novel as well as most film renditions. This is a great misfortune. To exclude the historical commentaries; or the digressions on argot, religious faith, and the sewers; or passages concerning Cosette's early enslavement by the Thénardiers, Marius's penurious circumstances, and the band of young revolutionaries who die on the barricades is to rip the hero's moral struggles out of the context that gives them meaning. It is to transform *Les Misérables* into something like *Le Misérable*, to reduce a vast fresco of individual and collective destinies into the relatively trite tale of an ex-convict on the run.[1] Hugo's poetic imagination ceaselessly weaves analogies between Jean Valjean's spiritual progress and humanity's striving toward freedom, harmony, and social justice. What we lose, then, through external abridgment or our own impatience to get on with "the story" is the highly uncommon interconnectedness of the whole. *Les Misérables* did not originally strike critics as dangerous because of its outlaw protagonist, nor was it initially banned by the Vatican for its plot. Even today, it continues to press for radical social reform, for national and international concord, by appealing for direct popular action that would bypass established institutions. In this chapter and the next, we will explore Hugo's interweaving of story and history—past, present, and future—by examining Les Misérables first as a historical novel, then as social and political satire, and finally as a collective romance.

Taking up the challenge of his great literary idol, Sir Walter Scott, Hugo had become the first French historical novelist at the age of 21 with the publication of Hans of Iceland (1823), set in late-seventeenth-century Norway. The Slave-King (1826), a haunting account of the 1791 slave revolt in Santo Domingo, soon followed, and the evocation of medieval Paris in The Hunchback of Notre Dame (1831) crowned his early ventures in the genre. It is not surprising, then, that despite the 30-year gap, his next major work of fiction would also be a historical novel. The intimate relationship for Hugo between story and history—both of which are called l'histoire in French—remained a constant throughout his career. The ostensible time frame of Les Misérables ranges from the first part of the 1700s to the workers' riots of June 1848, with the year 1815 functioning as a kind of watershed.[2] Indeed, the first sentence of Part 1 begins, "In 1815" (1); Part 2 opens by evoking the battle of Waterloo; the opening of Part 3 revolves around Marius's relations with his father, a hero of the Napoleonic campaigns; and Part 4 quickly brings up the fall in 1830 of the Bourbon monarchy, which had returned to power after the collapse of the First Empire (1804–15). For Hugo's readers in 1862, the text would have been firmly anchored in a not-so-distant past—if not their own, then that of their parents or grandparents. The feats of Napoléon's army would, at the very least, have been handed down as a modern-day legend. Some readers would have had vivid memories of the French Revolution, whether as children, advocates, or opponents. More recent developments mentioned in the text—the July Monarchy (1830–48), the 1832 insurrection, the Revolution of 1848—would have held personal memories for many others, echoes from younger days by which the present might, presumably, be measured.

Within this historical framework, Hugo forges links between his hero, the Revolutionary period from 1789 to 1815, and the doomed insurrection of 1832, links that considerably widen the scope of the novel. The association of Jean Valjean with Napoléon Bonaparte, for example, is clear from the outset. The ex-convict strides onto the stage of *Les Misérables* "on the evening of a day in the beginning of October, 1815" (59), thereby "appearing" in the year that the emperor "vanishes." Not only is he, at "forty-six or -seven" (59), the same age as the fallen ruler; to ensure that the comparison is not lost, Hugo adds, "he was entering Digne by the same road that, seven months before, the Emperor Napoleon had taken from Cannes to Paris" (60). The sublime fictive outlaw, Jean Valjean, shares a parallel destiny with the sublime political outlaw, Napoléon Bonaparte—the upstart usurper who had propagated the Revolution throughout Europe, much to the dismay of the reigning monarchies. When we later learn that Napoléon's victory at Montenotte as the general of the army of Italy was proclaimed in Paris on the precise day that Jean Valjean was shackled to the "great chain . . . riveted at Bicêtre" (84), the symmetry between them is complete. In 1796, the one begins his rise to power while the other plummets into penal servitude, that abyss of anger, malice, and despair. In 1815, the mirroring effect is repeated when the ex-convict undergoes a spiritual conversion soon after the ex-emperor has been exiled to the tiny island of St. Helena.

The digression on Waterloo, which immediately follows Madeleine's downfall and the death of Fantine, thus has bearing not just on French history, but also on the fate of Hugo's characters. Certainly the pack of allied armies that at last manages to corner Napoléon and cut him down foreshadows the police hunting party that, in "A Dark Chase Requires a Silent Hound" (II.v), brings Jean Valjean to bay outside the Petit-Picpus convent. Javert's "campaign" (476) against the fugitive replays Wellington's strategy, but with different results. The resemblances between the English general and the policeman, on the one hand, and between Napoléon and Jean Valjean, on the other, are an especially effective mechanism for coupling the story to history. Like Javert, Wellington is "impassive" and "coolly heroic" (318), a warrior who trusts to calculation rather than imagination. Both are models of "precision, foresight, geometry, prudence, . . . obstinate composure, imperturbable method, . . . war directed watch in hand, nothing left voluntarily to chance, ancient classic courage, absolute correctness" (345). In other words, both put their faith in themselves. The Englishman's strictly scientific approach to battle (*precision, geometry, method, watch*) recalls the description of Javert as a "conscientious, clearheaded, straightforward, sincere, upright, austere, fierce man" (204); it also prepares the great scene of the inspector's conversion and demise in "Javert Off the Track" (V.iv). Confronted by the incontestable moral superiority of Jean Valjean, "the fireman of order, the engineer of authority, mounted on the blind iron horse of the rigid path" (1326), finds himself as derailed from his former purpose in life as Saul of Tarsus on the road to Damascus (Acts 9). But, we recollect, Saul was transfigured by his glorious revelation into Saint Paul. Javert cannot reconcile his book of rules with the vision that opens before him: he prefers death to having to choose between "two roads, both equally straight" (1320).

Although, as Hugo points out, Napoléon "blundered" (476) no less in Russia than Javert in pursuing Jean Valjean and Cosette through Paris, this comparison extends no further. The emperor's genius— "intuition, inspiration, a military marvel, a superhuman instinct; a flashing glance, a mysterious something that gazes like the eagle and strikes like the thunderbolt, prodigious art in disdainful impetuosity, all the mysteries of a deep soul, intimacy with Destiny; . . . faith in a star united with strategic science" (345)—is of another order entirely. Here, Hugo's discussion of Waterloo recapitulates the traits of his out-law hero. By the end of Part 1, the reader has already glimpsed the "mysteries" of Jean Valjean's "deep soul" in the Champmathieu affair. During his journey of faith to Arras, "[s]omething was pushing him, something drew him on" (240), the narrator explains, setting up the equation between the transcendent acts of moral conscience and Napoléon's "superhuman" dialogue with Destiny. By the end of Part 2, the convict's gift of "inspiration," his "flashing glance," and his lightning-like movements also stand revealed when he manages to invent a means of escape from Javert's ambush. As he flees with Cosette through the labyrinth of Parisian streets, "[i]t was as though he too were holding someone greater than himself by the hand" (448). His faith in something beyond himself is, like the emperor's, absolute and unquestioning.

The point of the dual analogy between historical and fictional figures is perhaps less evident. Why would Hugo use Javert and Jean
Valjean to reenact the adversarial relationship between Wellington and
Napoléon Bonaparte? Consider for a moment how differently the two
struggles end. As we have noted, the ex-convict symbolically fills the
empty place of the emperor on the stage of history. Since, in Jean
Valjean's case, the greater genius prevails over the lesser, one might
infer that he does not simply *replace* Napoléon, but that he represents
some form of progress over his predecessor. Correcting Napoléon's
final "blunder" at Waterloo by triumphing over Javert, he may help to
advance the cause of humanity first launched by the Revolution of
1789 and then exported to the rest of Europe by the imperial army.
The emperor's subsequent wrong turn into hubris, tyranny, and military disasters may be rectified, if not redeemed, by another tack of history altogether.

A closer look at the digression on Waterloo confirms this
approach. Though a stunning defeat for the French nation, the battle
constituted, for Hugo, only a momentary setback. In fact, he argues in
"Should We Approve of Waterloo?" (II.i.17), Napoléon's loss was
France's victory. At first glace, the true winner was "Counter-
revolution" (349), that is, the combined effort of the monarchies to
"clea[r] the decks for action against the indomitable French
Revolution" (348). But it became instantly clear to the Bourbon
Restoration (1814–30) that a return to the pre-Revolutionary status
quo was impossible. The dream was "finally to extinguish the volcano
of this vast people, twenty-six years in eruption" (348). The reality was
that the "crater" (349) at the center—the city of Paris—was ready to
explode if some civil liberties were not granted. Ironically, "since the
empire was despotic, royalty . . . was forced to become liberal, and
. . . a constitutional order has reluctantly sprung from Waterloo, to
the great regret of the conquerors. The fact is that revolution cannot
be really conquered, and that . . . it keeps reappearing, before
Waterloo in Bonaparte throwing down the old thrones, after Waterloo
in Louis XVIII granting and submitting to the charter" (348–49).
Napoléon had begun his career by spreading the Revolution beyond
France but then had turned despotic. The despots who replaced *him*

had to restore some civil liberties in order to command a sufficiently broad power base among the French people. The lesson: nothing can stop historical evolution toward freedom, because everything—whether voluntarily or involuntarily—serves its cause.

Thus, even the psychological effects of the national debacle were by no means wholly negative. Because "Bonaparte fallen seemed higher than Bonaparte in power" (352), a brand-new generation came to embrace both the Napoleonic past and a future called Liberty. Waterloo had rendered progress through military means impossible; the workings of revolution now had to operate otherwise. "The swordsmen are gone, the time of the thinkers has come" (349), we are told—a restatement of the claim several pages earlier that Goethe and Byron have brought far greater glory to Germany and England than Blücher and Wellington. "A vast rising of ideas is peculiar to our century" (344), in France as elsewhere. The brilliance of the humble pruner Jean Valjean, reflecting the genius of the "Corsican of twenty-six" (345) who in 1796 had conquered Italy, is that of the French people itself—"twenty-six years in eruption" (348) as of 1815, and still going strong.

The old system yields to the new. Revolutionary ideas pass, as if apostolically, from Robespierre to Napoléon to Jean Valjean. Given the location—right after the Champmathieu affair—of Hugo's analysis of Waterloo and its consequences, one might wonder whether the emperor's fate does not illuminate the ex-convict's as well. How, for example, are we to view the hero as the new symbol of social progress when he has just abandoned his thriving community in Montreuil-sur-mer to return to prison? Again, Madeleine's ruin is implicated in Napoléon's through the notion of loftier glory. The mayor's sublime self-sacrifice is, for the reader at least, hardly a moral defeat. One could even say that, not unlike Bonaparte, "[Madeleine] fallen seemed higher than [Madeleine] in power" (352). The setback in Jean Valjean's life, as in the cause of collective progress, is only temporary. Or, better yet, the setback for *Madeleine*, as for Napoléon, is permanent. But *Jean Valjean* will continue to advance, along with the French nation.

A symbol of the enormous human potential of the poor, the uneducated, the outcast, Jean Valjean demonstrates how far a properly enlightened soul might venture in its search for perfection. By the same token, the self-imposed law of conscience is related not only to Napoléon's unerring military sense and ability to create new legislative codes; it also represents, for Hugo, the superior principles of revolution that ensure the issue of a higher order out of civil chaos. To engage in revolution is to break the law, to overthrow the existing legal system, in the name of a social ideal. Recurrent political upheaval—the periodic eruption of revolutionary fervor—thus corresponds in the novel to the repeated paroxysms of the hero's conscience. Conversions are spiritual revolutions; revolutions are social conversions. So, when Jean Valjean discovers Cosette's love for Marius in "The Blotter Talks" (IV.xv.1), he experiences a "frightful uprising" that parallels the concurrent insurrection of 1832: "What are the convulsions of a city compared to the émeutes of the soul? . . . Every gulf had reopened within him. He too, like Paris, was shuddering on the threshold of a formidable and obscure revolution" (1148). Jean Valjean's lifelong quest for inner harmony replays the epic struggles of the French nation to achieve unity and concord. Each "convulsion of the conscience" (224) that marks his enduring moral transformation is analogous to renewed political strife in the name of a higher good. No matter what we may have already accomplished, "[w]e are never done with conscience" (1387), the narrator insists, just as humankind will have no permanent social rest until it has fully established the utopian future.

Passages that link Jean Valjean with revolutionary France are scattered throughout *Les Misérables*, most notably in the digressions on "Argot" (IV.vii), on the inevitable forward course of civilization in "The Dead Are Right and the Living Are Not Wrong" (V.i.20), and on the luminous potential of the Parisian spirit in "Paris Atomized" (III.i). We remember the outlaw's ability to solve his ethical dilemmas, for instance, when Hugo claims that "[i]mmense combined thrusts rule human affairs and lead them all . . . to equity. . . . [Humanity's force] is scarcely dismayed by those contradictions in the posing of problems that seem impossibilities to the vulgar. . . . In the meantime, no halt, no hesitation, no interruption in the grand march of minds" (1000). The spirit of the law that serves as Jean Valjean's moral compass, so the text implies, governs severe turbulence at the national level as well. The collective drive toward social justice guarantees that, over the long run, selfish forms of government will give way to more equitable systems.

This law of progress, by which the entire species "makes the great human and terrestrial journey toward the celestial and the divine" (1236), both justifies right-minded failures and remedies momentary digressions from the correct historical path. As we observed in Napoléon's case, events sometimes seem to run counter to long-term social aims. The narrator reopens the question of historical evolution when he connects the ill-fated 1832 insurrection with Waterloo by alluding to the battle in his description of the barricades, as well as to the "N" (1083) formed by the streets in which they are erected. Once again, however, the issue of collective setbacks is resolved in conjunction with Jean Valjean's own reversals. Thus, in extolling the "disinterestedness" and "stoic disappearance" (1238) of the insurgents, the text recalls the hero's "disinterested and stoical" (1153) attitude toward loss—even, it turns out, in matters of love. The rebels' valiant self-sacrifice is equated with Jean Valjean's self-abnegation in saving Marius for Cosette, just as Waterloo was earlier equated with the Champmathieu affair.

In this way, the story line of the novel sheds new light on history. The convict's submission to the imperatives of conscience helps us see the glorious side of humanity's worst moments. To lose in one sense is to triumph in another. What counts, above all, is the lesson in courage: "To strive, to brave all risks, to persist, to persevere, to be faithful to oneself, to grapple hand to hand with destiny, to surprise defeat by the slight terror it inspires, . . . to hold fast, to hold hard" (592), is to set a radiant example for individuals and nations alike. Instead of responding to catastrophe with despair or derision, the narrator declares, we must admire those who fall—like Madeleine, or Napoléon, or Cambronne, or the young revolutionaries—while "struggl[ing] for the great work with the inflexible logic of the ideal" (1238). Because exemplary self-sacrifice inspires others, progress does not require an unbroken chain of advances. On the contrary, it is noble defeat that supplies the impetus for some of our greatest leaps forward. Accordingly, Hugo suggests, the grand utopian goal of "harmony and unity," of "universal peace" (1236), will one day be realized, confounding the reactionary forces that may hold it in abeyance, but that will never prevail.

In thus intertwining microcosm and macrocosm, story and history, Jean Valjean's fate with that of his country, Hugo imposes a hidden order on his sprawling work. As with history itself, even the most digressive developments can be viewed as partaking of an organic whole. The autonomous, self-governing hero obeys the precepts of conscience alone; revolution follows its own self-imposed dictates—the mysterious, inexorable "logic of the ideal" (1238)—rather than prescribed legal codes; the novel unfolds along multiple axes, all converging on the notion of progress. At one point, the narrator states that the text, which turns upon a "social outcast," has *"Progress"* as its true title: "The book the reader has now before his eyes—from one end to the other, in its whole and in its details . . . —is the march from evil to good, from injustice to justice, from the false to the true, from night to day, from appetite to conscience, from rottenness to life, from brutality to duty, from Hell to Heaven, from nothingness to God. Starting point: matter; goal: the soul. Hydra at the beginning, angel at the end" (1242). Each part of the novel, regardless of its subject, enters into an internally coherent system. From the emphasis in this passage on life, light, and heaven, we are to infer that French history, like the convict's story, is headed toward "the celestial and the divine" (1236).[3]

In addition to its thematic function, history also plays a very concrete role in the work. To enhance the verisimilitude of his occasionally improbable plot, Hugo grounds it in a wealth of historical details. Although by no means a realist novel in the tradition of, say, Balzac's *Le Père Goriot* (1835; *Old Goriot*) or Flaubert's *Madame Bovary* (1857), *Les Misérables* reflects a number of techniques that inscribe its timeless, mythical dimensions within the familiar frame of modern, post-Revolutionary civilization. It is not surprising to find such a balance of realism and romance in the work of the self-appointed heir to Walter Scott. As we might well recall, the romantics were the first to use local color—that is, particulars regarding the speech, behavior, and surroundings of a given region or period—to supply realism to works of fiction. In realist writers, recourse to archival research for such details shifted to close observation of the world around them. The romantics, generally speaking, wrote historical novels about other times and places; the realists employed similar methods to characterize contemporary society.

Within this context, *Les Misérables* presents several particularly striking features. First, it draws on local-color techniques typical of both realism and romanticism, blending the author's research with his personal observations and the testimony of others to evoke the not-so-distant French past. Thus, for example, Hugo's reconstruction of the battle of Waterloo, or "The Year 1817" (I.iii.1), or the Paris sewers, that "Intestine of Leviathan" (V.ii), relies on external documentation. So does "Argot" (IV.vii), his digression on the language of villainy, whereas his account of life in the Petit-Picpus convent derives from Juliette Drouet's memories of monastic education. Many other descriptions, however, acquire their accuracy and immediacy largely from the writer's own experiences: the layout of the battle site at Waterloo; reminiscences of the Bastille elephant commissioned by Napoléon and of the "strange moment in contemporary history" (624) represented by the royalist salons during the Restoration; Marius's apprenticeship in poverty and his political evolution from monarchism to republicanism; the assessment of Louis-Philippe and the July Monarchy in "A Few Pages of History" (IV.i); the events of "June 5, 1832" (IV.x), including the ordeal of "[o]ne observer, a dreamer, the author of this book, who had gone to get a close view of the volcano, [and] found himself caught in the arcade between the two fires" (1065); the streets and neighborhoods of Paris before urban development under the Second Empire (1852–70); and the phenomenal barricades assembled during "the fatal insurrection of June 1848, the biggest street war history has ever seen" (1169).

The interjection of an authorial voice in such passages contrasts sharply, of course, with the realist aesthetic of impersonal observation. Yet the accumulation of details likely to reverberate, to a greater or lesser extent, in the reader supports Hugo's claim of depicting the experiences of "many minds of our time" (630). His tale is embedded in fundamental facts and truths that can be recognized and shared by a much broader community. If we add to the novel's multifaceted historical verity its psychological realism—the deterioration of Fantine's personality, Champmathieu's muddled thinking, the dangers inherent in Marius's seduction by reverie, Thénardier's inability to understand any mind-set but his own, Jean Valjean's quasi-incestuous emotional investment in Cosette, Cosette's post-pubescent awakenings—we see that the romantic novelist of *The Hunchback of Notre Dame* (1831) has, by 1862, taken a few pages from his realist contemporaries. One might even say that, far from undercutting the mythical power of Jean Valjean's story, Hugo's realist touches heighten it by implicating the reader in the issues they pose.

The spillover in *Les Misérables* between story and history, myth and reality, does not, however, end here. Lest we think it an easy matter to distinguish between the two interwoven strands, we need to reexamine the use of local color. For Hugo presents as authentic evidence a host of spurious "documents" and "facts" not only in the plot but also in his historical digressions. The proliferation of notes and messages in the story line itself begins to blur the boundaries between truth and fiction. Mlle Baptistine's epistles describing her brother; Myriel's budget; the recording of Madeleine's dream on an envelope; Fantine's missive to Thénardier, delivered by Jean Valjean; the testament of Marius's father, Colonel Pontmercy; Thénardier's swindling letters; Marius's meditations on love; Eponine's warnings; the script on Cosette's blotter; Javert's resignation—all appear as purely invented writings aimed at developing the characters or moving the narrative along. But as texts within a text, they operate much the same as the "real" documents that Hugo also mentions. Cosette is no less transformed by Marius's manuscript, for instance, than is the young man by the copy of Napoléon's *Mémorial de Sainte-Hélène* (1823), the old issues of the *Moniteur,* and the other "histories of the Republic and the Empire" (630) that effect his political conversion. By the same token, Hugo "reproduce[s]" (359) fictive articles about (the phony) Madeleine's arrest and condemnation published by genuinely existent papers—the *Drapeau Blanc* and the *Journal de Paris*—the latter of which embellishes its account with "facts" the reader knows to be false. When, at the end, Thénardier exhibits the clipping on Madeleine from the *Drapeau Blanc*, along with one from the *Moniteur* on Javert's demise, as evidence to support his wholly erroneous reading of Jean Valjean, the merging of the real and the imaginary is complete.

Finally, in turning to passages that purport to be historically accurate, we find that they cannot always be taken at face value. Sometimes Hugo simply fabricates his information. In the "History of Corinth Since Its Foundation" (IV.xii.1), whose title playfully suggests a serious study on ancient and modern Greece, the narrator describes the location, history, appearance, ambience, and occupants of a fictitious tavern in the Marais; he even goes so far as to report the inscriptions that adorn the nonexistent walls and doorway. Given the true-to-life representation, one cannot avoid reading the chapter as if it were a faithful reconstruction, on a par with the bird's-eye view of the quarter itself (IV.xiii.2). At the same time, not all maps in *Les Misérables* are equally reliable. Consider the chase scene through the Petit-Picpus neighborhood. Though no current map retains any trace of the area, the narrator maintains, it is "shown clearly enough on the map of 1727, published in Paris by Denis Thierry, Rue Saint-Jacques, opposite the Rue du Plâtre, and in Lyons by Jean Girin, Rue Mercière, à la Prudence" (453). Yet despite the realist trappings, the map, like the quarter itself, never existed. They are no more "real" than Jean Valjean—who, of course, is no less "real" than any other verbal construct. However assertive it may be, historical discourse can never recapture the past; it can only reconstitute a fragment here or there, based on the data available. It must therefore be seen as hypothetical, open to question, ever fluid and revisable.

Sometimes Hugo underscores the interpretative nature of history by inserting a scrap of obviously invented material into an anecdote, thereby rendering the rest suspect as well. Amid the recollections of "A Few Pages of History" (IV.i), the chapter "Facts from Which History Springs and Which History Ignores" (IV.i.5) offers any number of documents, dialogues, and other "revealing facts" (845) that would be difficult to verify. One coded message, we are told, contains the letters "*u og á fe*, which was a date, and which meant *this 15th April*, 1832" (848). But since this is also a play on words, *Hugo a fait* (Hugo made), one is hard-pressed to accept the remainder of the message as authentic. Suddenly, other details in the same chapter—the letter fragment, the encrypted list of insurgent leaders, the recipe for gunpowder—also seem less than trustworthy. Where does fact leave off and fiction begin? Or, for that matter, can fiction not contain a greater measure of truth than fact? If the interpenetration of story and history in *Les Misérables* reveals the writer's playfulness, rhetorical mastery, and intellectual range, it also challenges his reader to regard *all* official versions of history with suspicion—and to seek the reality behind the appearance.

6

Back to the Future

The appeal of Hugo's historical novel to a contemporary audience does not reside only in its multilayered reflection on the past. To remember what has since been effaced, to conjure up the glories of long ago, to look for meaning and direction in the lessons of earlier evils or sacrifices, is to speak in some way to present events. Let us recall for a moment the author's situation in 1862: the most famous writer in the world—who had served in the upper and lower houses of the French parliament from 1845 to 1851—had by now spent 11 years in the Channel Islands as a political exile from Napoléon III's Second Empire. That life on English-speaking Guernsey's 25 square miles was a far cry from his former days is, to say the least, an understatement.

Hugo was not in any way a stranger to polemic and satire. He had delivered fiery speeches to the National Assembly in support of workers' and children's rights; had engaged in political pamphleteering under the Second Republic (1848–52); and, in his opening address as president of the international Peace Congress assembled in Paris in August 1849, had become the first person on record to advocate the idea of a "United States of Europe."[1] He also had an established reputation as a literary polemicist. In *The Slave-King* (1826), he had attacked the fundamental racism, self-serving rhetoric, and general narrow-mindedness of both colonialist "Revolutionaries" and leaders of the slave uprising in Santo Domingo. His third novel, *The Last Day of a Condemned Man* (1829), was a powerful indictment of capital punishment.[2] And the short narrative *Claude Gueux* (1834) had focused on the evils of the French criminal justice system. More important, the exiled poet had sharpened his skills in political invective in a series of works directed at Napoléon III and his cohorts: in *History of a Crime* (1851; published in 1877), *Napoléon the Little* (1852), and *Châtiments* (1853), he had poured out, in prose and in verse, a searing condemnation of Louis-Napoléon Bonaparte's rise to power, coup d'état, and continued support by the bourgeoisie. By 1862, his anger had not lessened but had taken a new tack. Unless he expressed such views more covertly, his novel had little chance of achieving blockbuster status in his own country, much less of avoiding outright censorship—that is, being banned—by a repressive regime. The trick was to illuminate recent history, to exalt the republican socialist ideals of 1848 and denounce the usurper's hedonistic reign, without directly mentioning either topic.[3]

For the alert reader, Hugo throws down the gauntlet on the very first page, in the brief preface cited in chapter 3. Society has created "a hell on earth" (xvii) for the victims of ignorance and poverty: men are degraded by stultifying work at low wages; women sell their bodies to feed themselves and their families; children are physically abused and spiritually starved. By implication, the author commits himself to solving these "three problems of the century" (xvii) by dedicating his book to the cause of social and political change. The goal is to transform hell into heaven on earth, the Second Empire into the next iteration of the French Republic. The wider audience for such a conversion may well be the rest of the world and future generations—who, Hugo dreamed, would one day enjoy the peace and prosperity of a universal Republic.[4] But his immediate concern is to touch the social conscience of his fellow citizens and to galvanize them into action.

Three times in the course of the novel he reminds us plainly of this goal—the noble objective of the Revolution of 1789 and of the 1832 insurrection as well. Within the first 40 pages, the dying Revolutionary

G. defends the bloody struggle to overthrow the old order. He did not himself vote for the death of the king, he says, because "I do not believe I have the right to kill a man, but I feel it a duty to exterminate evil. I voted for the downfall of the tyrant, that is, for the abolition of prostitution for woman, of slavery for man, of darkness for the child" (39). This speech, coming so soon after the preface, confirms and highlights the author's own radical agenda. Later, in "A Few Pages of History" (IV.i), the narrator refers twice to the republicans' effort in 1832 to renew, if not improve upon, the social program of their political forebears. "To the rights of man, proclaimed by the French Revolution," we learn, "they added the rights of woman and the rights of the child" (840). By the 1830s, the earlier focus on guaranteeing civil liberties for adult males had expanded to include proposals for bettering the condition of women and children, too. As in 1789, violence became a means to attaining a higher end. The republican socialists may have been savage in their pursuit of a better world, but they were "barbarians of civilization" (854), aspiring to nothing less than "work for man, education for children, an amenable social climate for women, . . . bread for all, ideas for all; the Edenization of the world, Progress" (853). Already, they have made progress by recognizing the inalienable rights of all citizens, regardless of age or gender—a position, we should add, championed by the Revolution of 1848 and then by Hugo himself, in his capacity as a representative to the Legislative Assembly.

His book now aims to perpetuate the work of previous generations, to make revolutionary history relevant to the present, to revive the great dream: "Progress" (853, 1242). To those who might deem fiction an insubstantial art, and reading literature a frivolous pastime, he issues a veiled warning. Although ostensibly delineating the virtues of prayer in his "Parenthesis" (II.vii) on monastic life, the narrator targets other modes of meditation as well. "There is no labor, perhaps, more useful" (522), he declares, than reflecting on "the will of the infinite, that is to say God" (519). In understanding where the universe is headed, we can make much more fruitful use of our own lives. "Contemplation leads to action" (519), he continues. It tells us where to put our practical energies; it keeps our gaze fixed on the ideal; it is a tool of progress.

What may not be evident to the English-speaking reader is that this desire to be "useful" (in French, *utile*) again refers to the preface: "so long as ignorance and misery remain on earth," it concludes, "there shall be a need for books such as this" (xvii; *des livres de la nature de celui-ci pourront ne pas être inutiles*, literally, books such as this cannot be useless). Writing a great work of literature does not just mean creating something beautiful (as the proponents of "art for art's sake" would argue); it also serves the cause of progress by providing a "model" (520) of the ideal that others can emulate. Far from being unimportant or unnecessary, art helps to elevate the human race, to place it in greater harmony with the infinite. Reading likewise resembles contemplation: "A man is not idle because he is absorbed in thought. There is a visible labor and there is an invisible labor. To meditate is to labor; to think is to act" (521). Becoming mentally engaged with his novel is, in Hugo's view, but the first step toward social and political engagement. "Turn your book facedown and you are in the infinite" (518), he remarks in the same chapter. His work is a springboard into the realm of eternal values.

The question of progress posed by the collective setbacks of the earlier part of the century thus comments on more recent events. The response to the section "Where Are They Going?" (IV.ix), about some of the main players on the 1832 barricades, might well be: where are we now, and where are we headed? In light of the march "from evil to good, from injustice to justice, . . . from appetite to conscience, from rottenness to life, from brutality to duty, from Hell to Heaven" (1242) that Hugo says his book represents, the answer is simple enough. The present is hell—a notion confirmed by the preface—and an especially grotesque version at that. To reach its heavenly future, the "soul"/"angel" will have to liberate itself from the "matter"/"Hydra" (1242) in which it is mired. If we read *Les Misérables* as a tale about the here and now—our own as well as the writer's—many of the themes, images, and characterizations pertaining to days past take on a new significance. The same is also true of the visionary passages, to be examined in chapter 8, relating to humanity's more sublime future. Between his portrayal of France from the First Republic to the July Monarchy and his conception of the world to come, Hugo launches a potent satirical offensive against the Second Empire. He indicts the present both by condemning past ills that, in fact, have yet to be eradicated and by promoting his vision of a better tomorrow. In a two-pronged attack, he shares his dream of a utopian future that will replace its reverse image, the dystopian past/present. The grotesque will, with appropriate intervention, give birth to the sublime. In undermining the reader's own complacency, the text becomes a strident wake-up call.[5]

In the midst of the Second Empire's neoclassical revival, then, *Les Misérables* wields like a club the romantic aesthetic principle of the grotesque. A world whose taste runs to order, coherence, proportion, and regularity is confronted, page after page, by representations of the deformed, the monstrous, the unnatural, the incongruous, the imperfect. Even today, the novel retains the power to shock. It may no longer be possible to react with puritanical horror to either Cambronne's response—"*Merde!*" (341; literally, shit)—to the English general's demand for surrender, or to the narrator's glorification of such verbal defiance. But the elaboration of this motif in connection with the Paris sewers is considerably more repulsive. (Can one really dwell for long on the thought of wallowing through the muck, much less almost drowning in it?) Other passages depict the forces of social disharmony at work: the suffering of the poor and the innocent, the miscarriages of justice, the callous indifference of the well-off—all enter into a dystopian system.

Exploiting a broad spectrum of grotesque images, Hugo develops his vision of hell on earth and associates it with present-day France. Let us examine some of these satirical strategies, with particular attention to the ways in which the analogy between past and present emerges in the text. For the victims of society mentioned in the preface, degradation—physical, psychological, or spiritual—always results in twisted features or behaviors. Jean Valjean spends his youth "in rough and poorly paid labor" (83), trying to support his sister's seven young children. When, in the winter of 1795, every source of work dries up, he steals a loaf of bread and ends up in prison for 19 years. Under the penal system, he is transformed "by a slow numbing process [from] a man into an animal" (91). He undergoes a complete regression. Crushed beneath the "frightening accumulation of laws, prejudices, men, and acts, . . . whose weight appalled him" (92), the gentle-hearted laborer is metamorphosed into something hardened, monstrous, and evil. "Can man, created good by God, be made wicked by man?" the narrator asks. ". . . Can the heart become distorted, contract deformities and incurable infirmities, under the pressure of disproportionate grief, like the spinal column under a low ceiling?" (89). The answer clearly is yes. The disaster of an unjust sentence, which presumably wipes out his family in the process, seems to write itself into his very bones. He wears his prison brand both inside and outside.

Years later, other characters display similar signs of abuse. In 1823, the "bristling hair" and the "wild restless eyes" (265) of Champmathieu, Jean Valjean's prematurely aged look-alike, remind him of how he had looked the day he entered Digne, "full of hatred, and concealing in his soul that hideous hoard of frightful thoughts" (266) accumulated in prison. Champmathieu recounts, in notably inelegant language, his backbreaking labors as a wheelwright and his daughter's equally miserable existence as a washerwoman. "Her husband used to beat her. She's dead. We weren't very happy" (272), he summarizes. Without her pitiful income, he had become homeless, hungry, and incarcerated on suspicion of stealing an apple. When Jean Valjean and Cosette observe the passing of the chain gang in 1831, we see that criminal justice has not evolved since the previous century. Whether innocent or guilty, all have been leveled by disgrace into a foul procession that resembles one huge, snarling, mindless beast: "Their thoughts appeared on their faces; the moment was appalling; demons visible with their masks dropped, ferocious souls laid bare" (909). Those who may not have been evil before going to prison have been remolded by the experience—a reminder of the hero's earlier sufferings that reinforces the extraordinary nature of his conversion. As in a *danse macabre*, the dance of death, they make up a veritable gallery of grotesques: "there were the facial angles of every beast, old men, youths, . . . cynical monstrosities, . . . savage grimaces, insane attitudes, snouts set off with caps, . . . faces childish and therefore horrifying, thin skeleton faces that lacked only death" (909). The implication—that these are the living dead—does not put the convicts into a special category. On the contrary, they exemplify the plight of all outcasts, dehumanized by society as the faceless masses.

For women, the trap of poverty can lead to prostitution, that promiscuous intermingling of bodies without names. On the barricade, Enjolras pleads for a few volunteers to leave before the slaughter, in part to help protect women. Because, in 1832, men are the primary breadwinners, their lives guarantee the innocence of the women who depend on them. They have no right to sacrifice themselves for abstract causes if the result will be more concrete suffering: "And those of you who have daughters, and those who have sisters! . . . Young girls who have no bread, that's terrible. Man begs, woman sells. . . . There's a market for human flesh; and it's not with your ghostly hands . . . that you can prevent them from entering it!" (1183–84). Their fathers and brothers dead, the girls may well fall into misery, prostitution, prison. Going on to lament the lack of educational opportunities for women, a situation that perpetuates their dependent—and hence highly vulnerable—status, the rebel leader effectively recapitulates Fantine's experience a decade earlier. Her story, that of "society buying a slave" (187), is but a variation on this motif of the human flesh market.

The lovely Fantine had known neither father nor mother, bearing from the outset "the mark of the anonymous" (122) on her brow. Abandoned with a small child by her first lover, Tholomyès, she must earn enough money for two while concealing the fact that she is an unwed mother. When she cannot make ends meet after a meddling bigot gets her fired, she first sells her hair to pay for Cosette's care and then her teeth as well. Quite literally, her social conditions dismember her. The sacrifice is horrific: as she smiles, "the corners of her mouth were stained with blood, and there was a black hole where her two front teeth had been" (186). She sinks ever deeper into misery, her fate strangely paralleling Jean Valjean's. The convict is "distorted" (89) by prison; the poor "cannot go to the far end of their room or to the far end of their lives, except by continually bending more and more" (186). Like him, she works for a pittance—when she can. In her new job, she sews 17 hours a day for 12 sous (or 60 centimes). But "a contractor who was using prison labor suddenly cut the price, and this reduced the day's wages of free laborers to nine sous" (186). In an ironic twist, wretches like Jean Valjean are used by the competitive capitalist system to create even more widespread social misery. Only the contractor, who produces nothing at all, makes a fortune.

When Fantine's creditors howl aggressively at her door, she feels hunted down, and "something of the wild beast began to develop within her" (187). Her increasing panic and coarseness echo Jean Valjean's reversion into an "animal" (91), again highlighted in the chain gang scene. Unable to meet their demands or to feed the Thénardiers' frenzy, she sells her only remaining asset, her body. Hugo's imagery of the void tracks her decay. From the "black hole" (186) in her mouth to the rental of her private space to her burial in the common grave, her fate seems grimly consistent: "She was thrown into the public pit. Her grave was like her bed" (300). In just a few short years, she loses love, beauty, and life itself, demeaned and disfigured to the point of martyrdom by the indifference and cruelty of others.

The next generation in *Les Misérables* fares no better. Born in 1815, Cosette feels that she had begun life in "a pit," that her childhood was a time "when there were only centipedes, spiders, and snakes around her" (890). This nightmarish scenario is a remarkably accurate recollection of her early existence as the Thénardiers' domestic slave: "something like a fly serving spiders" (382). For the children of poverty, life is a bad dream from which one rarely wakes up. Relentlessly punished, beaten, and mistreated, the little girl has a face that expresses the "habitual anguish seen in the condemned and the terminally ill" (399), that is to say, in a Jean Valjean or a Fantine. She is destined, it would seem, either to die young or to join the ranks of society's reprobates. Before the age of six, "[i]njustice had made her sullen, and misery had made her ugly" (157). Like the galley slave, she is all too aware of being treated unfairly and, like him, she is warped by resentment. At eight, her expression suggests that she will become "an idiot or a demon" (400). She lives under a table, fed there on leftovers with the dog and cat; she lies to avoid punishment; and she plays with a small lead sword, cutting off flies' heads or cradling it like a doll. Whether as demon or idiot, her future seems anything but bright. The realist details stress both her humanity and the external, social, and therefore wholly preventable nature of her suffering. When Jean Valjean buys her labor at a vastly inflated price so she can spend the rest of the day at leisure, he inverts the kind of greedy mentality that had drained him, Champmathieu, and Fantine dry—and that had settled on Cosette as its next victim.

The horror merely shifts to the Thénardiers' own children, who end up in Paris exploited by those responsible for protecting them. The daughters, Eponine and Azelma, contribute to the family finances through petty theft and prostitution. Neither children nor girls nor women, they have been reduced by misery to a "species of impure yet innocent monsters" (738). Their abnormality is not simply moral. By 1832, the 16-year-old Eponine has lost her youth to "the hideous old age brought on by debauchery and poverty" (737). The narrator does not shield us from the brutal details. This "pale, puny, meager creature" (736) is one of the living dead. With her "bony shoulders protruding from the blouse, a blond and lymphatic pallor, dirty shoulderblades, red hands, the mouth open and sickly, some teeth missing, the eyes dull, bold, and drooping, the form of a misshapen young girl and the stare of a corrupted old woman" (736), Eponine assumes Fantine's ghastly features, but at an even younger age.

Gavroche rescues the little Magnon boys, his own brothers rented out for profit and now hungry and homeless. But his domicile in the belly of the Bastille elephant is hardly the place for boyhood dreams. The elephant's "gigantic skeleton" (958)—another reminder of the hungry poor—harbors hordes of rats as well. Once the lights go out, the rodents swarm over the wire cage that encloses the bed, "smelling there what the good storyteller Perrault calls 'some fresh meat'" (963). As in so many fairy tales, by Perrault and others, reality quickly takes on a terrifying cast. The "mice" ate his cat, Gavroche explains, and would not hesitate to eat them all, too. The image of little boys being eaten alive is shocking; but, as the text shows, it is just a metaphor for what happens to far too many children—and their parents—day after day, year after year, in real life. Hugo's "nightmare of social tyranny" (Frye, 238), with its mad, demonic, tortured, incarcerated, swallowed-up wretches, stands with Dante's *Inferno* (1321) and Orwell's *1984* (1949) as a haunting representation of human anguish.

Back to the Future

The dismal, lurid, grotesque imagery with which Hugo consistently depicts *les misérables* from the 1790s to the 1830s drives home a powerful point. Despite all the talk about progress, nothing changed for a large swath of humanity. Conditions may have improved for some individuals and their offspring. But each new generation of the poor and uneducated faced the same physical, psychic, and moral disintegration. But what of more recent times? Since the last chronological date in the text concerns the June 1848 barricades, we might hope to find there some orientation regarding the future. The Saint-Antoine barricade, we learn right away, was "monstrous" (1171). Built from the ruins of several massive houses, it presented "a menacing fraternization of all rubbish. . . . It was the acropolis of the ragamuffins. . . . The fury of the flood was imprinted on that misshapen obstruction. What flood? The mob. . . . There was something of the cloaca in this redoubt, and something of Olympus in the jumble. You saw there, in a chaos full of despair, . . . a howling upheaval, and those thousand beggarly things, the rejects of even the beggar, containing fury and nothingness alike. . . . It was a garbage heap, and it was Sinai" (1171–73). Constructed by the underclass of the next generation (*ragamuffins, mob, beggar*), the barricade is no less repulsive than its brutish creators (*monstrous, rubbish, fury, misshapen, cloaca, jumble, chaos, howling upheaval, fury, nothingness, garbage heap*). Other details of this description further link the anger and despair of the June insurgents with the men, women, and children who populate Hugo's story line, set in earlier years. Given the failure of the workers' revolt in 1848 and the subsequent political backlash, the text points toward continued misery for the have-nots in the future.

At the same time, the evocation of garbage and cesspools recalls Jean Valjean's symbolic death and resurrection in the sewer, itself a figure for the untold potential of society's rejects. The sublime will emerge, "all dripping with slime" (1298), from the grotesque; redemption will come from below. Those who have, Christ-like, sunk lowest will stand highest (*acropolis, Olympus, Sinai*), capable of delivering a new law to the French nation. The apocalyptic overtones of the passage (*flood, howling upheaval*) likewise indicate that, for Hugo, modern revolutions are impelled no longer by the middle class but by legions of neglected discontents gushing forth from the abyss. The sewer thus represents far more than the hero's triumph over the worst elements in himself, the capacity for evil that might still erupt at any time. As society's collective unconscious, the sewer is also the pit of shared hypocrisy and repression, a dark, unspeakable, unexplored place where the comfortable and well-off attempt to relegate whatever might disturb their peace of mind.

One need only read the delightfully disgusting depiction of past "floods" (1263) from the sewer to perceive the satirical aim of the novel's cloacal imagery. Before 1789, the narrator maintains, Paris could manage neither her moral nor her material affairs, "nor sweep away her filth any better than her abuses. . . . Men could no more succeed in orienting themselves in [the sewer's] channels than in understanding themselves in the city; above, the unintelligible, below, the inextricable; . . . Labyrinth underlay Babel" (1263). The two domains—city and underworld—were related in form and content. As the capital grew haphazardly above, its grotesque replica stretched out in tandem below. But social abuse and moral corruption under the ancien régime rendered it as foul as the sewer itself. The unstemmable tide of revolution thus found its counterpart in inundating filth: "At times this stomach of civilization had indigestion, the cloaca flowed back into the city's throat, and Paris had the aftertaste of its slime. These resemblances of the sewer to remorse had some good in them; they were warnings, very badly received, however; the city was indignant that its sludge should have so much audacity, and did not countenance the return of the excrement. Drive it away better" (1264). While posing as a history of the sewers, Hugo's description of such periodic excremental eruptions celebrates what Freud would call the "return of the repressed"—society's underdogs—not just in 1789, but in 1830, 1832, and 1848. Terms like *remorse, indignation,* and *audacity* underscore the human faces behind the "floods." Paris has occasionally choked on the "aftertaste" of its own wastefulness.

Despite some cosmetic tinkering, social conditions may be no different in 1862. To convey this bleak message, Hugo weaves a tapestry of covert clues. Beginning in 1805, the narrator declares, an obscure hero named Bruneseau succeeded in mapping, cleaning, and reconstructing the labyrinthine sewers. These engineering efforts continue, moreover, to the present. According to the statistics furnished, each successive government—including "the existing régime" (1271)—had a hand in extending the underground network. As the only explicit remark about the Second Empire in the entire text, the reference indissolubly links Napoléon III's reign to the sewer. By situating this association under the rubric of "Future Progress" (V.ii.6), Hugo further connects it to the book's overarching theme of progress. His reading of past history in *Les Misérables* also gives him insight into contemporary events.

Logically, the sewer functions as the focal point for Hugo's shadow history of the Second Empire, since the sewer itself is the city's hidden double, the place where all secrets stand revealed: "The history of men is reflected in the history of cloacae. . . . Each thing has its real form, or at least its definitive form [in the sewer]. . . . Here, no more false appearance, no possible plastering" (1260–61). From masks and false noses to Falstaff's vomit to evidence of murder to Marat's shroud, nothing escapes exposure. "A sewer is a cynic. It tells all" (1262); and so, presumably, will Hugo. Indeed, scrutinizing the capital's underside can provide a new slant on current politics. For, the narrator claims, uncleanliness has a refreshing sincerity about it: "When a man has spent his time on earth enduring the spectacle of the grand airs assumed by reasons of state, oaths, political wisdom, human justice, professional honesty, the necessities of position, incorruptible robes, it is a consolation to enter a sewer and see the slime that befits it" (1262). In other words, the grandeur of political rhetoric is, for the most part, just verbal excrement. Only later, with historical hindsight, can most of us see it for what it really was. Reminding the reader of his extensive experience in government both making and listening to speeches, Hugo asserts his credentials for recognizing sleaze and slime when he sees them.

So, when the historical digression on the Paris sewers shifts to a discussion of their present condition, we are alert to underlying meanings. Thanks to Bruneseau, we are told, "Today the sewer is neat, cold, straight, correct. . . . It is comely and sober; drawn by the line; we might almost say neat as a pin. It is like a contractor [or rather, a supplier; in French, *fournisseur*], become a state councilor. We almost see clearly in it. The filth behaves decently. . . . Do not trust in it too much, however. Miasmas still inhabit it. It is more hypocritical than irreproachable. . . . In spite of all the processes of purification, it exhales a vague odor, suspect as Tartuffe after confession" (1269–70). Beneath the neat appearance, the sewer still stinks (*vague odor*). It can never fully disguise what it is. Once more, the theme of duplicity *(hypocritical, suspect, Tartuffe)* appears in conjunction with politics (*state councilor*). The notion of a large-scale supplier attaining membership in the French Council of State might not strike twentieth-century Americans as unusual—just a case of upward mobility. But the Conseil d'état is no ordinary advisory board: it is the nation's supreme judicial body, specializing in administrative and constitutional law. The image, then, evokes someone who could never properly fill such an appointment and hence who could only look ridiculous in the role or get to play it by fraudulent means.

The allusion to Louis-Napoléon, that sham emperor, sheds light on developments elsewhere in the novel, and vice versa. The sewer's "cold, straight, correct" (1269) lines, for example, echo the description of the neighborhood around the Gorbeau tenement. Located at 50–52 Boulevard de l'Hôpital, the structure stands against a distinctly dismal backdrop: "everywhere, parallel rows of trees, buildings in rigid lines, . . . long, cold perspectives, and the dreary sameness of right angles. No variation in the terrain, not a caprice of architecture, not a wrinkle. Altogether, it was chilly, regular, and hideous. Nothing is so stifling as symmetry. . . . There is something more terrible than a hell of suffering—a hell of boredom" (432). Previously, we saw that the sewer had evolved as a grotesque reflection of the city's chaotic layout above. Now, the text goes one step further. The architectural order imposed on the infernal underworld, beginning with the First Empire, is matched in 1823 by the dystopian configuration of streets and buildings on the outskirts of Paris.[6] There is even a "smell of sulfur" (431) in the air to reinforce the hellish connotations.

One might well expect such a setting for the building where various *misérables*—Jean Valjean and Cosette, the Thénardiers, Marius— will live at one time or another. But Hugo aims his portrayal of hell on earth at the Second Empire as well. Inserting itself into history with the December 1851 coup d'état, Louis-Napoléon's regime is immediately signaled by the numerical gap in the tenement address. When the narrator goes on to disparage the neighborhood's severe appearance, unbroken lines, geometric regularity, and monumental proportions, we recognize Hugo's attitude toward the contemporary revival of the neoclassical aesthetic.

More specifically, he deprecates Baron Georges Haussmann's ongoing urban reconstruction, authorized in 1853 by Napoléon III. Over the next decade and a half, Haussmann transformed Paris into a modern showpiece by widening the streets, creating the tree-lined *grands boulevards*, adding and remodeling parks, erecting a magnificent opera house, building bridges and train stations, installing a circular railway, and, not coincidentally, improving the sewer system. The cost in human and artistic (not to mention fiscal) terms was enormous. Haussmann's town planning required razing many districts, widely admired for their picturesque quality, that also housed the working and nonworking poor. (Baudelaire allegorizes this urban displacement in his poem "Le Cygne" [1861; "The Swan"], dedicated to Hugo.) In numerous chapters, the narrator imaginatively "restores" the ancient streets and neighborhoods as he follows Jean Valjean's itinerary.

The book thus becomes a veritable travelogue for a city that no longer exists and that the exiled writer must reconstitute from memory: "Through demolition and reconstruction, the Paris of his youth, that Paris he devoutly treasures in memory, has become a Paris of former times" (446). Each recollection is an opportunity to point out what has been lost. We therefore learn about the intricacies of the old Marais, only to be told, "[t]he Rue Rambuteau has devastated all this" (1083). Even the fictive Petit-Picpus quarter has been "completely blotted out" (453) by new construction. "Progress" under the Second Empire has, one might say, been but a destructive illusion. It has defaced an infinitely varied and uniquely beautiful city, driven the nation's foremost poet abroad with other militant republicans, and forced the underprivileged out of their homes and into remote enclaves as "dreary," "hideous," and "stiffling" (432) as the Gorbeau district.

Hugo's satire of Napoléon III's grandiose projects—projects that would help to ruin the empire financially—has yet another important dimension. The "exile" of the poor to the outskirts of Paris was not simply an accidental side effect of urban development. Rather, in the opinion of the government's enemies, it formed an integral part of a plan: to dislodge from the city center the inhabitants most likely to riot, if not to instigate full-scale revolution; to destroy the twisting, winding, unpredictable byways that had previously lent themselves to erecting and defending barricades; and to assure crowd control by constructing long, wide, rectilinear avenues conducive to speedy troop deployment. Neighborhoods like those glorified in *Les Misérables* that might foster popular uprisings had thus been triply deactivated. Just as society in the novel "represses" the wretched—Jean Valjean, Marius, Thénardier—by pushing them into the sewer, so had the Second Empire marginalized its underclass by evicting it from the city.

From this perspective, the characterization of the contemporary cloaca as an Haussmannesque creation, where "[t]he filth behaves decently" (1269), conveys several meanings. On one level, it calls attention to Louis-Napoléon's fundamental hypocrisy. Beneath the semblance of imperial leadership, one finds nothing but excrement. On another level, producing well-behaved "filth" encapsulates the motivation, not only of tidying the system below, but also of reordering the unruly masses above. This, Hugo implies, is what parades as "progress."

Considering that the text contains a shadow history of events beyond 1848, the reader would have grounds for wondering whether any of the main characters might be viewed as a figure for Napoléon III. After all, as we have observed, Javert is compared with Wellington, and Jean Valjean is closely allied with Napoléon Bonaparte. As the most familiar occupant of both the Gorbeau tenement and the Paris sewer—Marius and Jean Valjean are, by comparison, just passing through—Thénardier would seem the most logical candidate for pairing with the emperor. The innkeeper's inflated view of himself and devotion to flimflammery of every sort strengthen the case for seeing him as a vehicle for commenting on the French leader. The one "Tartuffe" (1270) serves to unmask the other.

Hugo tones down the biting satire of *Châtiments* (1853), which portrays the Second Empire as a kind of Tinseltown and Louis-Napoléon as a political bandit in disguise.[7] But he provides plenty of hints that Thénardier can be read as the emperor laid bare. He thereby simultaneously avoids the danger of official censorship and devises a genteel, teasing mystification that involves each of us in the making of meaning. Such guessing, discovering, and (re)creating all heighten the pleasure of reading. Early on, the villain's plasticity, slipperiness, megalomania, and "pretensions to literature and materialism" (378) identify him with the traits commonly attributed to Napoléon III by his enemies. The self-proclaimed "fellowsopher" (378; *filousophe*, literally, swindler-sopher)—a word play on "philosopher"—pontificates as he empties others' pockets. Later, in the Gorbeau ambush, he adds the "pretty little romantic beard" (768; *barbiche*, that is, goatee) that decorates the familiar imperial visage embossed on French currency and caricatured in the papers. By the close of the novel, Thénardier virtually parades his alter ego through the "statesman's clothing" (1437) that he rents before visiting Marius.[8]

A born scoundrel, Thénardier continues to degenerate to the end, functioning as a dark, regressive force on those whose lives he touches. From the moment he is introduced, we understand that nothing will ever change him for the better. As the narrator puts it: "There are souls that, crablike, crawl continually toward darkness, going backward in life rather than advancing, using their experience to increase their deformity, growing continually worse, and becoming steeped more and more thoroughly in an intensifying viciousness" (153). The image is scarcely flattering. Along with Louis-Napoléon, who reversed historical progress by dismantling the Second Republic, Thénardier epitomizes moral decay and spiritual deterioration. He may look perfectly presentable, but his soul is monstrous. In short, he belongs in the sewer.

The correlation of Thénardier, Napoléon III, and regression, on the one hand, and of Jean Valjean, Napoléon Bonaparte, and progress, on the other, suggests one additional layer to Hugo's reading of contemporary history. Might not the passages pertaining to the glorious military leader camouflage a critique of the ignominious nephew?

Hugo had already contrasted the two emperors and their empires in *Napoléon the Little* (1852). A subtler approach in *Les Misérables* would involve simply not designating one term of the comparison. Such a strategy would explain the repeated references to 1815, both direct and indirect, as a way of gesturing toward the reverse date, 1851.[9] It would also clarify Thénardier's bogus link to the Napoleonic legend, established well before the historical digression in Part 2.

In an ironic turn, the innkeeper enters the novel almost literally under the sign of Waterloo—the painting that decorates the tavern in Montfermeil. But the illustration of his courage in battle is utter fiction: "This Thénardier, if we can believe him, had been a soldier, a sergeant he said; he probably had been in the campaign of 1815, and had even been brave, it seems. . . . The sign of his inn was an allusion to one of his feats of arms. He had painted it himself, for he knew how to do a little of everything—all badly" (154). Hedging his description with expressions of doubt (*if we can believe him, he said, probably, it seems*), the narrator indicates that the fabrication is not even clever. With its red blotches to signify blood and a smoky haze to represent the battle, the picture can be nothing but junk. Small wonder that Jean Valjean refuses to "purchase" it as the price of his ransom in the ambush, even though Thénardier tries to pass it off as an original by Napoléon's court painter. "David wanted to immortalize that feat of arms," he explains. "I have the general on my back, and I am carrying him through the storm of grapeshot. That is history" (797). Yet, as the reader knows, that is not history at all. Consistent with his behavior throughout the text, Thénardier unscrupulously rewrites events to his own ends.

According to Hugo, so does Louis-Napoléon. Capitalizing on the Napoleonic myth, the nephew has cast himself as heir to Bonapartist power and prestige. But like Thénardier's pathetic efforts to pass for an artist and a "statesman," the usurper of the Second Republic is a crude imitation of the illustrious original. Hugo turns Napoléon III's manipulation of the nation's mythologizing fervor against him by tacitly juxtaposing the other's exploits. The narrator conjures up the figure of Napoléon on horseback at Waterloo, spyglass in hand, asserting that "this whole image of the last Caesar is alive in the imagination" (312–13) of the entire world. Clearly, since he was the last of the line, the current "Caesar" (the title of all Roman emperors) can only be a fake. In fact, many would say that the dead ruler was more "alive" than his pale descendant. Marius's impassioned speech to his friends about Napoléon's multifaceted genius condemns the present emperor by the implied contrast. "He had in his brain the cube of human faculties. He made codes like Justinian, he ruled like Caesar, his conversation combined the lightning of Pascal with the thunderbolt of Tacitus, he made history and wrote it, his bulletins are Iliads, he joined the figures of Newton with the metaphors of Muhammad. . . . He saw everything; he knew everything" (672–73), the young man says. Who could possibly compete with such hyperbole? Even Louis-Napoléon would not have thought to compare himself with Newton, Pascal, or Muhammad.

Napoléon can also be deemed the last Caesar—an abbreviation for the Roman dictator (Gaius) Julius Caesar, who had been a brilliant general—by virtue of his military prowess. Not solely in the digression on Waterloo does Hugo extol this aspect of Napoléon's "genius." In Part 1, he elaborates on two operations well beyond the demands of connecting Jean Valjean with the emperor. First, he recalls the excitement provoked throughout the region by Napoléon's return from Elba (which led to the recovery of his throne without the firing of a shot). Then he emphasizes an earlier triumph by heralding the announcement, on 22 April 1796, of "the victory of Montenotte, achieved by the commanding general of the army of Italy, whom the message of the Directory to the Five Hundred, of the second Floréal, year IV, called Buonaparte" (84). In Part 3, he recapitulates the history of the Revolutionary army by recounting the valor under fire of Marius's father, including the episode at Eylau where "the heroic captain Louis Hugo, uncle of the author of this book, sustained alone with his company of eighty-three men, for two hours, the entire force of the enemy's army. Pontmercy was one of the three who came out of that churchyard alive" (614). Hugo again interweaves fact and fiction, using eyewitness testimony to verify (and so enhance) the legend of the Napoleonic Wars while "corroborating" elements of the plot itself. When he subsequently depicts Marius's discovery of Colonel Pontmercy's brave deeds and, through him, of that "rising sun, Napoleon" (631), the reader can draw on this wealth of vivid textual experiences to imagine the young man's sense of wonder and admiration.

The catalog of dazzling victories and valiant defeats— Montenotte, Novi, Arcola, Marengo, Arcola, Günzburg, Ulm, Austerlitz, Hamburg, Jena, Wagram, Eylau, Friedland, Moscow, Beresina, Dresden, Wachau, Leipzig, Fontainebleau, Arney-le-Duc, Waterloo—reads like a map of Europe. The names are familiar; the myth is glorious. In 1862, the military campaigns under Napoléon III bore no such patina. Not that they had been wholly unsuccesful. France had allied itself with England, Sardinia, and Turkey against Russia in the Crimean War (1854–56) and again with England against China in the Anglo-Chinese War (1856–58) and in a follow-up expedition to Peking (1860) to enforce the treaty. Yet these shared triumphs seemed far less stirring to those who had to pay for them than those of the fabled past.

Recently, things had even gone badly on the battlefield. The clashes in June 1859 at Magenta and Solferino during the Franco-Piedmontese War against Austria (1859–60) had been huge bloodbaths that did not result in real victory. Worse yet, Napoléon III had been so disturbed at the sight of the carnage and apprehensive about the next steps to be taken that he had abandoned the war and signed a truce. His judgment may have been impeccable: the slaughter was sufficiently horrendous that the international Red Cross was founded in its wake. But when we remember that Hugo composed the last piece of Les Misérables in 1861 at the site of Napoléon's final defeat, we sense all the more poignantly the contrast between the two commanders-in-chief.

Finally, the writer launches his boldest offensive against the current regime under the guise of criticizing the First Empire. Despite Napoléon's brilliant mastery of war and government alike, something was missing. The lesson unfolds in the scene where Marius exalts Napoléon's wide-ranging genius to his republican friends. He concludes: "To be the empire of such an emperor, what a splendid destiny for a nation. . . . [T]o be for Europe a kind of golden people through glory, to sound through history a Titan's fanfare, to conquer the world twice, by conquest and by resplendence, that is sublime. What could be greater?" (673–74). The response from Combeferre, one of the revolutionary leaders—"To be free" (674; in French, *Être libre*)—takes him by surprise. Suddenly, the entire panegyric seems mere grandiloquence. Marius bows his head: "These cold and simple words had pierced his epic effusion like a blade of steel, and he felt it vanish within him" (674). Combeferre's brief words counter Marius's high-flown praise, expressed in sentences that run to 100, 150, and even 250 or so words.

Hugo's maneuver, tacitly aimed at the Second Empire, is double-edged. The central point concerns empires in general. No matter how great—and Napoléon's was perhaps the greatest ever—all fall far short of the republican ideal. The inference is that the reign of Napoléon III, who had illegally overthrown the newborn Second Republic, had done more than destroy the one "free" modern state throughout Europe and hence the highest form of civil life to which one could aspire. In addition, in return, Napoléon III could offer nothing but the pitiful shades of the First Empire and the first emperor. He is damned for not being Napoléon, who, as Marius's friends insist, was misguided anyway. A more covert message derives from the resemblance between Marius's epic sentences and the author's own 100-word, one-sentence preface. If we apply Combeferre's perspective to this passage, it can now be rephrased and understood in republican terms. "So long as there shall exist . . . a hell on earth"—because we cannot eliminate ignorance and poverty by extending equal rights through representative government—we need "books such as this" (xvii) to keep the true, democratic republican ideal alive. Hugo's work will not be "useless" (xvii) if it succeeds in refocusing the French nation on the preeminent goal: "To be free" (674).

As much as Hugo despised Louis-Napoléon, he was painfully aware that the problems in France could not be imputed to a single conniving individual or clique. The ruler's power base was, in fact, firmly rooted in the middle class. The nation had overwhelmingly elected him president in December 1848; he had had the satisfaction of winning by a vast majority the plebiscite held in late December

1851 to approve his coup d'état earlier that month; and a second plebiscite the following year had almost universally supported the proposal to establish an imperial form of government. In the poet's view, the reactionary bourgeoisie had crushed the masses in 1848 and later acquiesced in tyranny for purely selfish motives. It was eager first to preserve its own privileges by limiting those of the working class, and then to sustain a regime that was bringing prosperity by fostering rapid capitalist expansion. Far from lampooning just Napoléon III and his cronies in *Châtiments*, Hugo had also railed at the self-indulgent egotism and mindless conformity of his compatriots.[10] Needless to say, the volume had not been a best-seller. To reach a wider audience with *Les Misérables*, and so perhaps to ignite social and political change, he would either have to forsake a more generalized satire or find a way to communicate his outrage without offending the reader. The bourgeois were an important element of the reading public. How could he best educate them?

One of the traits of traditional fiction—the interaction of a range of well-defined characters—allows Hugo to build compassion for the poor and downtrodden while presenting those who oppress or neglect them in an unsympathetic light. We might even say that the one is a function of the other. As readers, we identify so readily with the victims of injustice or persecution that the author's indignation becomes our own. We side with Jean Valjean and Champmathieu against the legal system; with Fantine against Tholomyès, Mme Victurnien, Bamatabois, Javert, and Thénardier; with Gavroche and the little Magnon boys against the Paris shopkeepers; and, just maybe, with the revolutionaries against the government troops. Taken together, however, these cases might seem related only as examples of human suffering or, again, of *unnecessary* human suffering. That the agents of such affliction might be much like us, our loved ones, or our associates is considerably less evident. In other words, so much attention and feeling are focused on *les misérables* themselves that we may not notice other recurrent patterns pertaining to their plight.

Still, when the archvillain of the text, Thénardier, recycles a number of themes during his diatribe in the Gorbeau ambush, he points to a vicious community that greatly exceeds his band of underworld contacts. Rebutting Jean Valjean's observation that he is nothing but a bandit, Thénardier displays his credentials as both a genuine wretch and a genuine bourgeois:

> Bandit! Yes, I know that you call us that, you rich people! . . . For three days now I've eaten nothing. . . . [Y]ou have padded coats like archbishops, . . . you eat truffles, you eat forty-franc bunches of asparagus in January, . . . you gorge yourselves. . . . [Meanwhile] we feel the blood stiffen in our veins and the ice reach our hearts, and we say, "There is no God"! . . . But we will eat you! We will devour you, poor little things! Monsieur millionaire, know this: I have been a man established in business, I have been licensed, I have been a voter, I am a citizen, I am! And you, perhaps, are not! (796–97)

Beneath the self-serving speechifying of the swindler, we hear other familiar echoes. The allusion to profligate archbishops, the ethical nihilism, the theme of eating or being eaten—all recall a key scene at the beginning of the novel, the conflict of values between Myriel and the self-righteous, self-seeking senator from Digne. As we shall see, this early episode telescopes the bishop's constant censure of egotism and complacency in all their manifestations. It also anticipates the ungenerous behavior that typifies not only Hugo's scoundrels but also the majority of prosperous or relatively fortunate characters.

Thénardier's insistence on his firmly middle-class status thus implicates a wide spectrum of comfortable citizens who have no interest whatsoever in comforting those who are less well off. The villain is correct in surmising that Jean Valjean's civil standing is even more irregular than his own. But the underlying insinuation—that the man deserves to be a victim because he is in some way inferior—reflects society's view of the have-nots as nonpersons, unworthy of concern or consideration. The needier they are, the less they should be helped.

In this way, Hugo's shadow history of the Second Empire features an entire nation that has abdicated its responsibilities to the poor and uneducated in order to pursue its own goals and pleasures. As long as the money keeps rolling in, who cares about social justice? Now that *we* have achieved the tripartite Revolutionary goal of liberty, equality, and fraternity, we can forget about *them*. The only real progress that remains to be made is in the commercial, industrial, and financial sectors. Jean Valjean's endless sacrifices in his lifelong struggle for moral and spiritual perfection serve a double political function: to model the nation's relentless quest for unity and concord and, conversely, to impugn the veneration of things as they are.

It is significant that he should be converted by Myriel, who alone of the characters in Book 1 makes it his business to lance social evil wherever he finds it. The good priest blames "the strong, the rich, and the wise"—and, more specifically, the male power structure—for the faults of "the weak, the indigent, and the ignorant" (14). Society withholds the means for attaining knowledge and self-sufficiency, and then feels wronged when crimes are committed by the illiterate. The real dangers, he cautions, are not thieves or even murderers but our own "[p]rejudices" and "vices" (27). One of Myriel's prime targets is therefore the legal system. He castigates a public prosecutor's use of deception to trick a poor woman into betraying her equally hapless lover; he rejects capital punishment as "monstrous" (16); and he criticizes the tax on windows and doors, which forces the poor to live in foul, windowless huts, as lawful misdoing. "God gives light to men, and the law sells it" (12), he declares, satirizing in advance the ludicrous extra charges that Thénardier tacks onto his inn bills.

But the bishop does not merely reprehend the shortcomings of those who exercise authority. He also exemplifies benevolent actions and attitudes. To regions where the needy are "treated with severity," or people are "greedy for profits and rich crops," or families are "divided by questions of property and inheritance," or there are ruinous "legal disputes" (9–10), he cites high-minded solutions developed by neighboring regions. He trades his palace for the local hospital so it can accommodate more patients, lives on a tiny portion of his income and gives the rest away, comforts the bereaved and those condemned to death, finds work for the jobless, and opens his house to anyone in trouble or want. And he espouses "universal free education" (14) for one and all, regardless of class or gender, a rather astonishing viewpoint for 1815—or 1851. Through Myriel, *Les Misérables* offers a barrage of early illustrations, both positive and negative, that help shape the reader's judgment on later issues, events, and characters. The priest's kindness and integrity are, in this light, simply the reverse, utopian image of the egocentric convictions and social ills that surround him.

By the time he trades witticisms with the senator, we can already guess what he thinks of his interlocutor's "philosophy." Having seized on Myriel's request for a carriage allowance as proof that all clergy are "greedy and miserly" (7), the senator lacks credibility from the outset. Yet he performs a crucial function by revealing outright the various facets, not to mention the magnitude, of his self-centeredness. In putting Thénardier's approach to life in the mouth of a respected member of the establishment, Hugo automatically undercuts the mindset of every well-off character in the the text. One is left to wonder just how much success stems from ignoring "such obstructions as conscience, sworn testimony, faith, justice, and duty" (28)—from the sort of unscrupulous mentality that the narrator associates with the slime in the sewer. As Myriel comments, such thinking "comes from great depths, unearthed by specialists" (31). The reader is left to savor the scatological innuendos. The senator's devotion to pleasure, disdain of the poor, embrace of the survival-of-the-strongest, and ridicule of self-sacrifice and belief in the afterlife lay bare the soul of a heartless, amoral being: "There is neither good nor evil," he proclaims, "there is only vegetation. . . . I must eat or be eaten, and I choose to eat. It is better to be the tooth than the grass" (30). He is the quintessential subject of the Second Empire, preoccupied with avoiding pain and pursuing self-gratification. How foolish to concern oneself with anyone except family and friends when there is no reward for the effort in this world or the next. To enjoy one's own existence is all that counts.

The bishop responds ironically to the other's positivist logic and unabashed hedonism. "Those who have acquired this admirable materialism," he declares, "have all the joy of feeling irresponsible, of thinking they can calmly devour everything—high positions, sinecures, honors, power rightly or wrongly acquired, lucrative retractions, useful betrayals, delectable lapses of conscience—and that they will enter their graves with it all totally digested. How nice!" (31) The senator, Myriel recognizes, has found the means of rationalizing even the most dishonest acts. Interlacing the vocabulary of commercialism (*acquired, lucrative, useful*) with that of sensual pleasure and delight (*admirable, joy, feeling, devour, delectable, digested*), he unmasks the ruthlessness that permits one person to thrive at the expense of the larger community. In taking what by right should not fall to him, the man would "devour" his neighbor as zealously as the felons that populate Hugo's novel. His voracious materialism—to which Thénardier also has "pretensions" (378)—allies him with the army of consumers created by the modern industrial state. But, Myriel suggests, such heedless consumption may not be so easy to swallow in the hereafter.

The senator's candid divulgence of his "philosophy" and Myriel's perceptive rejoinder prepare the ground for many scenes in *Les Misérables* involving quite ordinary citizens. The greed behind Thénardier's ambition—"to get rich" (380)—propels not only the senator but, as Hugo would have it, the entire middle class. The commercial aspirations of the bourgeoisie thus parallel the physical hunger of society's outcasts. It is not a pretty picture. The wretched endure "the deep yearnings of the human animal toward gratification" (1002), yearnings that lead to envy, sadness, and want. The selfish, meantime, smother in their own excess: their world is delimited by "prejudices, the darkness of the education of wealth, appetite increasing through intoxication, a stultifying of prosperity, which deafens, a dread of suffering taken, for some, as far as an aversion to sufferers, an implacable satisfaction, the self so puffed up it closes the soul" (1002). Through terms related to bodily responses (*appetite, dread, aversion, satisfaction*) and sensory deprivation (*darkness, intoxication, stultifying, deafens*), the text indicates that success and fulfillment—the end of moral and intellectual striving—render *les égoïstes* as brutish in their own way as *les misérables*. The more the self expands, the less one is fully alive.

The two modes of appetite enter into conflict over the allocation of resources, with the have-nots reduced to begging for their very substance. Without generous action to redistribute some of the nation's wealth, the rich grow richer and the poor simply perish. But the middle class—broadly defined as "the contented portion of the people" (829)—has already achieved all the freedom it needs to attain its goals;

now it is bent on resisting further change. The narrator explains: "the bourgeoisie is the self-interest that has gained satisfaction. Yesterday it was appetite, today it is plenitude, tomorrow it will be satiety" (829). The grotesque imagery that depicts the sufferings of the flesh, as the destitute wither horribly and then vanish, has its counterpart in the gluttony of those who thrive.

It is not by coincidence that Thénardier begins his career as an innkeeper, bargaining in the necessities of food and lodging. His career in Montfermeil, we are told, resembles the secret life of many: "In an ordinary situation, [he] had all that is necessary to make—we do not say to be—what passes for an honest tradesman, a good citizen. At the same time, . . . under the operation of certain occurrences exciting his baser nature, he had in him all that was necessary to be a villain. He was a shopkeeper, in which a monster lay hidden" (422–23). Hugo's phrasing is damning, implying that, at best, such people can only *appear* to be respectable citizens. When the temptation grows too great, the monster bursts forth. By the end, the passage has established an indelible link between shopkeeping and villainy, part of an effort to persuade the reader that evil lurks in commercialism per se. The greater the lust for comfort and profit, the less honest or compassionate the dealings are likely to be.

The problem manifests itself not in one region but nationwide. In Digne, an exhausted and ravenous Jean Valjean finds himself refused at one cozy lodging after another, the locals' prejudice toward ex-convicts overriding his ability to pay—and his pleas for food, shelter, and water. In Montreuil-sur-mer, Fantine's creditors hound her mercilessly. The mean-spiritedness of the tradesmen is doubled by that of middle-class idlers, Mme Victurnien and Bamatabois, who have nothing better to do than make trouble. The young mother sells her "soul for a piece of bread" (187), a slave bought by society from cold, hunger, and privation. And since the legal system always sides with "a property-holding voter" against "an outlaw and an outcast" (191–92), regardless of the merits of the case, Fantine has no more chance of prevailing against injustice than Jean Valjean in Faverolles or Champmathieu in Arras. In Paris, the elderly scholar Mabeuf is victimized by the very booksellers he once frequented. When he must sell his precious collection piecemeal in order to eat, "they bought from him for twenty sous [or, one franc] what he had paid twenty francs for" (1045). A barber in his warm shop turns away the starving, sobbing Magnon children with a furious look; a baker tries to substitute second-quality bread for first, then speeds the boys' exit into the frigid streets once he has been paid; and a "potbellied bourgeois" (705) in the Luxembourg Garden, accompanied by a child who seems "stuffed" (1223), is not even aware of the famished creatures gazing longingly at his son's unwanted brioche.

In Hugo's opinion, the society that, in 1815, would ostracize and torment a former galley slave and, in 1832, two little boys, has continued to deteriorate. The 55 percent mortality rate for abandoned children cited by Enjolras on the barricade indicts a nation that spends less on the next generation than on beasts in the zoo, where contented citizens can take entertaining strolls with their own offspring—and where Gavroche steals the furnishings for his nightmarish "home" in the Bastille elephant. Compared with the "barbarians of civilization" who fight for a better future for all, the "civil advocates of barbarism" elegantly and politely fight for "the past, the Middle Ages, divine right, fanaticism, ignorance, slavery, the death penalty, and war" (854). In the halls of power, the decisions made every day to kill or suppress some while upholding the privileges of others have turned the clock backward toward real—rather than merely fictional—Gothic horrors.

As the text makes plain, the dichotomy between rich and poor, bourgeoisie and workers, those who live fully and those who barely exist at all, is but a logical extension of capitalist competitiveness. The economic law of the jungle undoes collective progress, mirroring the "intensifying viciousness" (153) that marks Thénardier's regression. The centrifugal forces that tear communities apart are apparent in Montreuil-sur-mer in the aftermath of Madeleine's disgrace: "there was that egotistic partitioning that follows the fall of great men—that fatal carving up of prosperous enterprises. . . . Jealous rivalries arose. . . . From that time on, everything was done . . . for gain rather than for good. There was no longer any center; competition and venom on all sides. . . . With [Madeleine] fallen, it was every man for himself; the spirit of strife succeeded to the spirit of organization, bitterness to cordiality. . . . [B]ankruptcy followed. And nothing was left for the poor. Everything disappeared" (361–62). With the possibility of personal gain in mind, no one cooperates with anybody else, and everyone's prosperity evaporates in the process. Greed kills some and destroys all. Pockets of prosperity vanish not just because people are by nature egotistic, but because there is no overarching system to provide for the indigent when individual benefactors depart. In the absence of any outside rescue organization, the reverberations from even localized financial disasters can be catastrophic. Thénardier's despicable aphorisms—"selfishness is the law of the world. . . . Every one for himself. Interest is the motive of men" (1439)—show their true colors in Montreuil-sur-mer. The lesson is a harsh one: no one profits in the long run from thinking only of self. The same may be said, the author indicates, for France as a whole.

The insurgents who rose up in June 1832, as in June 1848, to protest such inequities were themselves treated as "pariahs" (1235). According to the narrator, in these circumstances the people safely housed in the buildings that surround the barricades symbolically reject any commerce with the outside: "Let them get out of it themselves," goes the rationale for not enabling the trapped defenders to flee. "So much the worse for them. It's their own fault. They only got what they deserve. It doesn't concern us. Here is our poor street riddled with bullets. They're a bunch of good-for-nothings. Above all, don't open the door" (1235). Lumped with lawless villains, misunderstood by those whose long-term interests they serve, revolutionaries most often endure the same inhospitality as Jean Valjean in Digne or the Magnon boys in Paris. Hugo's snug—and smug—bourgeoisie is the opposite of Myriel, who receives from the poor the affectionate nickname Monseigneur Bienvenu, or "Welcome," in recognition of his open-door policy.

In a wonderfully comic passage, Marius's grandfather M. Gillenormand, himself a *grand bourgeois*, ridicules the mediocrity of middle-class aspirations. The bourgeosie may think highly of itself; the reality is repulsive. "In this century," the old man complains, "people do business, they gamble at the Bourse, they make money, and they are disagreeable [or, better yet, stingy; in French, *pingre*]. They care for and varnish their surface; . . . [but] they have in the depths of their conscience dung heaps and cloacas enough to disgust a cowgirl who blows her nose with her fingers. I grant these times this device: Nasty neatness" (1353). Beneath its prudishness and high-toned seriousness, the bourgeoisie is mean and miserly. It has been so preoccupied with polishing the exterior, that is, with appearances, that it has neglected the essential: doing something worthwhile with its money. Not only is it *misérable*, ensconced on the dung heap of its wastefulness; it has to answer for all the good it has failed to accomplish.

To be sure, the emphasis on prudery, frugality, respectability, and irreproachability targeted by Gillenormand would not be anachronistic in 1832. But for Hugo, the pharisaical embrace of these qualities corresponds perfectly to the repressive, authoritarian, formalistic mind-set of the Second Empire. (Such contemporaries as Charles Dickens, Elizabeth Gaskell, and Anthony Trollope parodied its analogue in Victorian England.) Instead of the Restoration or the July Monarchy, Gillenormand's harangue is directed at what the author considers a far more grotesque period in the nineteenth century. The "nasty neatness" of the self-satisfied, self-serving bourgeoisie, which persists in keeping Napoléon III in power, again bears a striking resemblance to the modern, Haussmannesque sewer. As with the other hypocrites in the novel, "The filth behaves decently" (1269)—but it is still filth. Humanity's forward "march" (1242) from the evils of injustice, falsity, appetite, rottenness, brutality, and matter toward heaven on earth begins with walking away from "business as usual."

It is important to appreciate the daring in Hugo's approach to awakening the reader's social conscience. Besides arousing compassion for society's outcasts and glorifying their untapped potential, the text satirizes the very mentality that it aims to "convert." The reader, after all, is almost by definition snug, comfortable, pleasure-seeking. Today, no less than in 1862, anyone sufficiently leisured and literate to enjoy a 1500-page work of fiction is one of the world's elite. (How often we forget that limited workweeks, child labor laws, even free, compulsory secondary education for both boys and girls did not become policies throughout Europe and the United States until well after the book's publication. It goes without saying that these policies are not always

enforced where they exist, and that they still do not exist in many corners of the world.) Yet the reader by no means comes away feeling sav-
aged. The setting of *Les Misérables* in earlier times, the subtle masking
of targets, the wide variety of voices employed, the dispersal of satirical content through both the story line and the digressions—all initially
veil the censure not just of "society" or of "the system" but of our own
lived values.

When the narrator calls the pursuit of happiness into question at
the end of the novel, we therefore tend to apply the remark first to
Marius's treatment of Jean Valjean: "It is a terrible thing to be happy!
How pleased we are with it! How all-sufficient we think it! Being in
possession of the false aim of life, happiness, how we forget the true
aim, duty!" (1428). Should not Marius, who has everything, take
greater pity on the ex-convict, who has nothing? But, we are immediately warned, it would be unfair to blame the young man for acting
out of ignorance. We may in fact recall that, during his recent confession, Jean Valjean himself had declared to Marius, "It is not enough to
be happy, we must be satisfied with ourselves" (1396). As the entire
text has argued, one must constantly choose between two opposing
forms of satisfaction: the one centered on self, the other on the rest of
humanity. Currently, Marius is focused on little beyond defending his
own interests and happiness, perhaps not unlike the reader.

This desire to enjoy one's existence is, the narrator says, both
understandable and universal: "The present has its excusable quantum
of selfishness; the life of the moment has its rights and is not bound to
sacrifice itself continually to the future" (1237). The here and now has
a legitimate claim on a portion (*quantum*) of our energies. By the same
token, collective progress must of necessity come to a halt when most
people restrict themselves largely to their own comfort. Individual
resistance to the needs of the human race can drag down a whole
nation. Personal appetite, multiplied by an entire population, can have
staggering consequences. "Matter exists, the moment exists, interest
exists, the belly exists," the narrator admits, "but the belly must not be
the only wisdom. The momentary life has its rights, . . . but the permanent life has its own as well. Alas! To have risen does not prevent
falling. We see this in history more often than we would wish. A

nation is illustrious; it tastes the ideal; then it bites the filth, and finds it good" (1241–42). In an obvious reflection on recent French history, several familiar themes resurface. Matter, self-interest, and the belly are identified not with *les misérables* alone but with their grasping middle-class counterparts. Civilizations, as well as individuals, can degenerate and become debased. Individual moral corruption leads to collective putrefaction. The sublime "ideal" of the Second Republic has given way to the grotesque "filth" of the Second Empire. Marius's personal journey is, as the novel closes, stuck at the same relatively unenlightened stage as is France in 1862. Some might say the same of the age of entertainment and consumerism in the last decade of the twentieth century.

The exiled poet's hope for his dissipated country is nevertheless apparent. Jean Valjean falls into evil and sin but, confronted with his wretched image after robbing a child, he redeems himself through a lifetime of self-abnegation. The French nation, too, has the potential to perceive its degradation and to make the sacrifices necessary to restore its moral stature. In "The Dead Are Right and the Living Are Not Wrong" (V.i.20), the narrator maintains that France has relapses of materialism that obstruct its supreme intellect with small-minded ideas. Yet its fundamental nature is still sound:

> The grandeur and beauty of France are that she cares less for the belly than other peoples; she knots the rope about her loins more easily. . . . She marches in the lead. She is a pioneer. That is because she is an artist. . . . [France] is Athenian via the beautiful, and Roman via the great. In addition she is good. She gives herself. She is more often than other peoples in the spirit of devotion and sacrifice. . . . A people, like a star, has the right of eclipse. And all is well, provided the light returns and the eclipse does not degenerate into night. Dawn and resurrection are synonyms. The reappearance of the light is identical with the persistence of the self. (1240–41)

Hugo's description is not, of course, a realist portrait but an idealized image of that great nation presently entrusted with the legacy of civilization passed on from Greece and Rome. Having held up a rather less flattering mirror to his country in other passages, he recalls here its critical historical mission, creative genius, and essentially generous spirit.

The message is transparent. France's past brilliance and glory will be that of its future as well—if only it can follow the examples of dedication provided, in *Les Misérables*, by Myriel, Fantine, Pontmercy, Jean Valjean, and the revolutionaries, and, in real life, by the "artist" (1240) himself. The alternative, he warns his compatriots, is degeneracy so complete that the beacon of moral, artistic, and intellectual vitality will be extinguished altogether. Like the hero in the sewer, they have touched the bottom and risk choking on their extravagance. Now is the time to throw off self-centeredness, to rewrite modern history as a collective romance, to "marc[h] in the lead" (1240) by once again showing humanity the way into the future.

The notion here of hitching up one's belt, ostensibly referring to growing leaner as one devotes more energy to others, carries another meaning as well: girding one's loins for battle. The "persistence" of Jean Valjean's sense of self through recurrent moral convulsions predicates the "resurrection" (1241) of France's true identity through renewed revolution. Beyond the romance and the satire, Hugo's great historical novel was, for the contemporary reader, nothing less than a call to arms.

7

Dramatic Conventions

As we have seen, the affiliation in *Les Misérables* between the personal and the collective underscores the epic proportions of Jean Valjean's fall and struggle for redemption. At the same time, the outlaw's ceaseless striving for perfectibility sharply criticizes the bourgeois status quo. Drawing on a wealth of themes and images associated with the heroic quest myth, Hugo depicts the desires and conflicts of the nation in terms of the individual. Such comparisons enable him to produce relatively abstract arguments about social and political issues from the more concrete experiences of his characters. We now turn our attention to yet another means of avoiding overabstraction: the use of theatrical conventions to maintain an atmosphere of confrontation and prepare its eventual resolution. A highly successful dramatist, Hugo knew how to please theatergoers. In *Les Misérables*, he invokes many schemas, practices, and techniques of the genre, and then plays off them in surprising ways.

That we have entered a *dramatic* universe—one characterized by conflict—is evident from the outset, when Myriel wrestles with his political contrary, the Revolutionary G., over the question of historical evil. The bishop's verbal jousting with the complacently materialist senator from Digne likewise helps set the scene for greater strife to come. Dramatic tension arises, simmers, and explodes in the various oppositions—between con artists and the police, psychological imperatives, social forces, aesthetic principles—that subsquently develop. In shaping these clashes through the conventions of melodrama, tragedy, and comedy, Hugo provides the reader with familiar tools for interpreting the range of dramas that unfold.

The most obvious references to the stage involve the "performances" occasioned by crime and punishment, and hence the novel's story line. Consider the motif of fictitious names and personas. Jean Valjean is like an actor who can play many different roles; his continual rebirths are marked by a proliferation of identities—24601, Myriel's "brother," M. Madeleine, Monsieur Mayor, 9430, Ultime Fauchelevent, "M. Leblanc," Urbain Fabre, Monsieur Jean—matched only by the shifting aliases of Thénardier and his cronies in the Patron-Minette gang. After leaving the convent, the fugitive hero stays one step ahead of the law by assuming the appearance of an ordinary, taxpaying citizen. Even his National Guard uniform is "a good disguise, which let him mix with everybody else while leaving him alone" (883). The villains' use of costumes and alter egos, on the other hand, adapts the tricks of the theatrical trade to illegal pursuits. Thus, in the dénouement, Thénardier plans to extort money from Marius by imitating the ex-convict's stagecraft. He rents a statesman's outfit from "the Changer," whose clothes "resembling as closely as possible, that of honest people generally" (1437), can transform a thief into a regular bourgeois. His penchant for illusion is already in evidence in Montfermeil, where the innkeeper reinvents himself as a "great actor" (417), playing up to his customers while robbing them blind.

But Thénardier's most imaginative intrigues are conceived in Paris, that grand social and political theater parodied by the "third substage" (718) of the underworld. Here, for example, he carefully arranges the scene of the Gorbeau ambush before his victim arrives and engages the members of Patron-Minette in supporting roles. The narrator observes: "Sometimes a play can be imagined from the cast of charcters: So, too, we can almost understand a band from the listing of the criminals" (725). In supplying both their rather nasty stage names

91

and their alternative aliases, Hugo implies that, in the criminal world as in world of spectacle, nothing is what it seems. The role is all.

The comparison is extended in his digression on argot, the secret jargon of evildoers: "Argot is nothing more nor less than a wardrobe in which language, having some bad deed to do, disguises itself. . . . It is apt for all roles, made squint-eyed by the forger, verdigrised by the poisoner, charcoaled by the incendiary's soot, and the murderer applies his red" (984). Ironically, language becomes grotesque in the service of felonious subterfuge, while the malefactors try to avoid suspicion by looking and acting as normal as possible. Argot deforms words to conceal meaning. Those who use it must likewise cloak themselves in deceit, hypocrisy, and rented outfits to obscure their ugly intentions.

Given the villains' penchant for theatricality, the task of the police is to unmask the culprits and close down the playhouse. Javert himself is not above putting on a disguise—say, that of a beggar—in the hope of identifying a fugitive from justice. Yet his preferred role is not that of actor but that of playwright. Rather than simply respond, after the fact, to criminal intrigues, he endeavors to encompass them in a master plot of his own. As Thénardier prepares to spring a trap on Jean Valjean at the Gorbeau tenement, Javert aims at ambushing the ambush. He tells Marius, whom he enlists as a spy next door: "Impossible for us to hide inside without the artists seeing us; then they would leave and break up the act. They're so modest! The public annoys them. None of that, none of that. I want to hear them sing and make them dance" (774). They will entertain the police with a variety show, confessing under interrogation and perhaps doing a jig for the hangman.

Much of the novel's suspense is generated by the cat-and-mouse games played by police, felons, and protagonists alike, with their secret identities, conspiracies, and counter-conspiracies. When the plot erupts into pursuits and confrontations—in the streets of Paris, the Gorbeau tenement, the exit from the sewers, Marius's home office— dramatic tension is at its height. As Aristotle first pointed out, the resolution of such climaxes produces intense aesthetic pleasure rooted in psychological relief.

Yet Hugo's art lies in rendering other modes of conflict no less gripping or satisfying than these collisions between heroes and villains, hunters and hunted. His forte of juxtaposing *moral imperatives,* for example, engenders electrifying scenes in such celebrated plays as *Hernani* (1830), *Lucrèce Borgia* (1833), and *Ruy Blas* (1838). In *Les Misérables,* the clash of good and evil on the social stage is repeated by the inner strife of a number of characters—Jean Valjean, Javert, Marius—and by their evolution toward a higher form of conscience. Their dilemmas transport the reader into genuine *psychomachias,* or internal divisions, over moral issues. Should the mayor and financial benefactor of Montreuil-sur-mer save a miserable wretch accused in his place by denouncing himself and returning to prison, or should he remain free to provide work and sustenance for an entire region? Should Marius help the man who rescued his father at Waterloo or the father of the girl he loves? Can the policeman, faced with the glorious revelation of a higher good, ignore the demands of the legal code and free his lifelong quarry?

In each case, competing voices split the personality into factions that war over loyalties, choices, courses of action. For Madeleine, the interior monologue actually becomes a dialogue between discordant personas.[1] In each case, the stakes are enormous, carrying life-or-death consequences for both the self and others. The human conscience, that "battlefield of the passions" (220), becomes a powerful force in the shaping of destinies. Little wonder that, for the reader, the conclusion of each anguished decision-making process has a cathartic effect.

The knotting and unknotting of the plot through dramatic junctures is likewise apparent in Hugo's treatment of social upheaval and military encounters. The epic struggles at Waterloo and on the barricades further punctuate the text, helping to create and sustain its sweeping rhythm through digression and story line alike. Although the reader already knows the outcome of Napoléon's campaign against Wellington, as well as of the 1832 uprising, neither episode lacks drama or suspense. Indeed, both ill-fated enterprises are depicted in theatrical terms. If civil war is "one of the fatal phases, at once act and intermission, of this drama whose pivot is a social outcast, and whose true title is *Progress*" (1242), so is the battle of Waterloo. The two historical misadventures are to be viewed as plays within a play, reflecting the whole of the novel while contributing to the development of the plot.

Thus, as we have noted, Jean Valjean's downfall in the Champmathieu affair is mirrored by the defeat first of Napoléon, then of the young revolutionaries. Likewise, the rout of the French army at Waterloo can be in part explained by the perfidy of the topography and of Napoléon's guide, that is, by an ambush worthy of Thénardier himself. By the same token, Hugo's narrative depends to some extent on what happens on both the Belgian plains and the Paris barricades. The narrator stresses, for instance, that "one of the key scenes of the drama we are telling hangs on [Waterloo]" (311), namely, Thénardier's accidental rescue of Marius's father, Colonel Pontmercy. And the dénouement of the battle on the barricade enables Jean Valjean to rescue its lone survivor and, in so doing, to lay the groundwork for the dénouement of the entire book.

One could hardly claim, however, that such connections generate the excitement of good theater in and of themselves. Another perspective is needed to create the illusion of a third dimension, filled with ongoing action. To this end, Hugo invites us to gaze with him upon historical events from the standpoint of the divine Dramatist. Coupling the long-range angle with hyperbolic language, he maintains that God had never arranged a "more striking contrast and a more extraordinary meeting" (345) than that of Napoléon and Wellington at Waterloo. The clash of their personalities, military styles, and armies was the stuff of high drama, a cataclysmic reckoning whose effects are, for the author, still being felt. Jean Valjean may be the "pivot" (1242) of his own tale. But on the immense stage of nineteenth-century history, Waterloo was the "hinge" (339).[2] The allusion to doors evokes the theatrical notion of blocking, by which the complex movements of characters on, off, and around the stage are managed. God's disposition of history's main players helps us make sense of unexpected disaster. Rather than representing a step backward for France, and for humanity in general, the "disappearance of the great man [after Waterloo] was necessary for the coming of the great century"

(339–40). History operates like a door, with pivotal events like Waterloo allowing one genius—in this case, Napoléon—to exit so that another might enter.

In a later passage on the timing of conflicts between "illustrious usurper[s]" (1053) and the historians who judge them, Hugo uses similar imagery to provide a clue regarding who the century's new star might be. Caesar and Tacitus, he asserts, are "two successive phenomena whose meeting seems mysteriously avoided by Him who, in staging the centuries, regulates the entrances and exits. Caesar is great. Tacitus is great. God spares these two grandeurs by not hurling them at each other" (1053). In other words, God protected Napoléon/Caesar from the scorn of Hugo/Tacitus, saving the writer's scourge for Napoléon III instead. As a result, he hints, the illusions of the Second Empire will follow those of the Bourbon Restoration (which had followed those of Napoléon himself): it will be "swept away . . . like a scene at a theater" (823) by forces beyond the present usurper's control. A version of Thénardier's cheap showmanship, the pomp and circumstance of Louis-Napoléon's regime are doomed to vanish in the next revolution that God is doubtless stirring up in the wings of history. The mighty wind of the poet-prophet's voice will help blast open the doors of illegitimate power and propel the French Republic back to center stage.

The metaphor of politics as theater, with God as the supreme producer and director, also permits Hugo to portray key moments in history in terms of spectacular natural events. Using the heightened language of the sublime, he compares the French Revolution, Waterloo, and the fight on the barricade to perilous storms, tempests, earthquakes, whirlwinds, and hurricanes, where some will perish and others prevail. The "thunderbolt" (40, 342) of battle or of social upheaval expresses divine judgment, simultaneously purging and purifying human affairs. The obvious analogy with Madeleine's "Tempest Within a Brain" (219) once again tightens the strands linking hero and nation, microcosm and macrocosm. The catastrophe that can strike down an individual—whether good or evil, saint or tyrant—is no less sensational than the one that can bring a whole country to its knees.

Besides referring to the dramatic aspects of *Les Misérables*, Hugo wields the conventions of melodrama, tragedy, and comedy to shape his tale. These theatrical conventions, which continue to underlie many plots on television and in the movies, should be recognizable today as well. In particular, the apparatus of melodrama—hidden virtue, sleazy villains, trials, recognition scenes, startling developments (or coups de théâtre)—dominates the story line. According to Peter Brooks, the problem of distinguishing good and evil in a post-Revolutionary world that had lost its defining measures spread from the unofficial theaters of the Boulevard du Temple to the works of major figures such as Hugo, Balzac, and Henry James.[3] A "low" theatrical mode that had enthralled popular audiences, the young author among them, during the first third of the century, thus passed into mainstream literature around 1830. For the reader of *Les Misérables*, of course, the principal excitement arises from the inability of the legal system, incarnated by Javert, to recognize Jean Valjean's fundamental virtue. An innocent man is persecuted while real felons continue to prey on the public. But the ex-convict is not the sole victim of the law. Fantine, Champmathieu, Cosette, the Thénardier children, Marius's revolutionary friends—all suffer from institutionalized oppression or neglect.

For this reason, Hugo can give a few delicious twists to the requisite trial scene, where "virtue misprized [is] eventually recognized" (Brooks, 27). Since it is not Madeleine but Champmathieu who is accused of being Jean Valjean, the hero cannot be vindicated. Rather, he must denounce himself in order to save his luckless namesake, a spectacular turn of events for those assembled. And when no one believes him, he must force the three witnesses who had previously misidentified Champmathieu to acknowledge *him* as Jean Valjean instead. In this way, the standard recognition scene, which establishes the identity and hence the intrinsic value of a misunderstood character, works to the benefit of Champmathieu but to the detriment of Madeleine. Despite—or because of—his genuinely radiant virtue, he will be condemned to return to the galleys. Champmathieu, too, is denied the public acclamation typical of melodrama. Too much life's victim to serve as a moral exemplar, he seems bound to end up in prison anyway for trespassing to steal fruit from other people's trees in order to eat.

While the Champmathieu affair provides perhaps the clearest illustration of melodramatic conventions in *Les Misérables*, Hugo continues to vary their usage throughout the text. In a marvelous comic moment that relieves the tension of the chase through the streets of Paris, Fauchelevent and "Madeleine" identify each other in the convent garden. For Jean Valjean to locate by accident the one place where he might safely hide with Cosette is a coup de théâtre worthy of any drama. So is the unanticipated gift of the silver he had stolen from Myriel; or his ability to produce a paper with Fantine's signature in order to rescue Cosette from the Thénardiers; or the scene in which he breaks his bonds in the Gorbeau ambush, burns his flesh with a red-hot chisel, and then throws away his only weapon, declaring, "Miserable people, . . . have no more fear of me than I have of you" (811); or when, in lieu of killing Javert at the barricades, he fires his gun into the air and sets his old enemy free.

One might also remark that Jean Valjean, Thénardier, Javert, and Marius are involved in intricately choreographed recognition games in both the Gorbeau tenement and the Paris sewers—games with tremendous consequences for them all. As the pieces of the puzzle at last come together in a recasting of the trial at Arras, Marius is able to recognize not just Thénardier, who fails to remember him in turn, but his father-in-law's sublimely moral nature. Bearing newspaper articles about Madeleine's true identity and Javert's suicide, the villain furnishes written proof that authorizes a new "reading" of the misunderstood Jean Valjean. As in melodramatic trial scenes, such concrete signs—including the scrap torn from Marius's coat—make the young man's world "morally legible, spelling out its ethical forces and imperatives in large and bold characters" (Brooks, 42). The many misreadings of the outlaw, and of *les misérables* in general, give way to a radically different construction. The jury's awe at Arras is so magnified in Marius that the ex-convict is revealed as a Christ figure: "An unparalleled virtue appeared before him, supreme and mild, humble in its immensity. The convict was transfigured into Christ" (1452). Although no public acclaim or rehabilitation awaits Hugo's hero, Marius ends by acknowledging his sanctity, first to Thénardier, then to Cosette, and finally to Jean Valjean himself.

The pervasiveness of these structures suggests that history might perhaps also be viewed as melodramatic. The literal fall of the imperial army into a sunken road, mirroring Napoléon's fall from divine grace, constitutes a sudden reversal of circumstances typical of the genre. Wellington's surprise victory at Waterloo thus becomes a coup de théâtre, along with the revolutions of 1830 and 1848 examined in various digressions—and the 1851 coup d'état passed over in silence. France was ambushed by a villain disguised as a prince, precipitating Hugo—a famous poet, former peer, elected representative, and member of the Académie Française—into the black hole of exile in the Channel Islands. But sudden changes of fortune may lie ahead as well. If the reader could but perceive the depravity of Louis-Napoléon/Thénardier and the merit of Hugo/Jean Valjean, then *Les Misérables* itself would play the crucial role of texts in other melodramas: it would condemn the one and justify the other before the bar of history.

Such a dénouement, whether it comes sooner or later, would belie the tragic reading initially invited by the novel. Plainly, almost everyone dies under pitiful conditions: Fantine, Gavroche, Eponine, Mabeuf, all of Marius's friends, Javert, Jean Valjean. Some survivors— for instance, the little Magnon children—may well not make it to adulthood or else grow up to be scoundrels. How could so much suffering, compounded by the hero's final martyrdom at the hands of his children, his pathetic, lonely end, and his unmarked, neglected grave, be considered from any but a tragic angle? Cosette and Marius, it would seem, effect one last dramatic reversal by showing up just in time to beg the dying man's forgiveness—only to forget him thereafter.

Still, Hugo's eclectic text contains so many comic facets that failing to take them into account as well might lead to a skewed interpretation. Beyond considerations of language itself, we can readily observe the manipulation in the text of stock comic characters and scenarios.[4] Some misreadings, we have seen, have dire consequences: Javert's exegesis of Valjean, the prosecution's portrayal of Champmathieu, society's view of revolutionary utopianism,

Napoléon's scrutiny of his destiny—and of the terrain at Waterloo. But others, especially those related to generational conflict or to the machinations of villainy, come straight out of traditional comedy.

Perhaps because of the universality of the generation gap, misunderstandings between young and old often appear in a humorous light. Marius reads his grandfather's inability to express his love as rejection; Gillenormand interprets Marius's devotion first to his father's memory and then to Cosette as youthful flings; Jean Valjean takes Cosette's tranquil demeanor for indifference to Marius and the young man's lovesick pursuit for a vile attempt at seduction. Such errors may have unfortunate results in the short run, but the scenes are played with gentle irony. So, when Gillenormand holds forth on the cowardice of the imperial army at Waterloo or the idiocies of republicanism, we laugh at his exaggeration: "The first whippersnapper you meet wears his goat's beard, thinks he is very clever, and tosses out his old relatives. That's republican, that's romantic" (696). The use of motifs that recall other "paternal" misjudgments—artistic as well as political— undercuts the reactionary mind-set in general, priming the reader to regard it as ridiculous in *all* its manifestations.

The "reading" blunders of the criminal element in *Les Misérables* are equally risible. Though Hugo's felons think themselves shrewd enough to fathom their intended victims while remaining impenetrable themselves, their plans can go amazingly awry. As in theatrical comedy, much of the action derives from mistaken identities. Montparnasse sneaks up on an old man to steal his purse, only to find himself flattened (and sermonized) by an old convict. The Thénardiers are lost in speculation about the "pauper"-"millionaire"-"robber" (408) who shows such kindness to Cosette in Montfermeil and who thwarts their every scheme to continue to use her as a cash machine. Later, in Paris, the former innkeeper again miscalculates in his dealings with Jean Valjean, both in the Gorbeau ambush and at the exit to the sewers. Because he assumes that anyone with something to hide is as unscrupulous as himself, Thénardier is completely outwitted on all three occasions. He plays the role of the duper duped (in French, the *trompeur trompé*) to the hilt, essentially fooling himself far more than anyone else. In the dénouement, he is again true to type. Mystified by Marius's inexplicable behavior, he unwittingly reveals the outlaw hero's salvational mission at the barricades while trying to gain the upper hand. In showing off to "Monsieur the Baron Pontmercy," he gives away the one secret from which he might have profited for the rest of his life.

As in comedy, then, nothing can prevail over true love. Neither (ig)noble fathers nor imposter villains succeed in impairing the match between Marius and Cosette. The alternative "happy ending" of the text—the triumph of the young couple, their reconciliation with the previous generation, and the crystallization of a new society around them, signaled by the wedding feast—is the mark *par excellence* of the comic plot (Frye, 163–64; Brooks, 32).

Yet, here too, Hugo offers a set of complex twists. Consider the convention whereby comedy tends to include as many people as possible in the final new society, centered on the triumphant son. In this scenario, "the blocking characters are more often reconciled or converted than simply repudiated. Comedy [nevertheless] often includes a scapegoat ritual of expulsion which gets rid of some irreconcilable character, but exposure and disgrace make for pathos, or even tragedy" (Frye, 165). At first, Thénardier seems to fit the role of the outcast perfectly. Thrown out of Marius and Cosette's home, the incorrigible scoundrel heads for America to take up a career as a slave trader.[5]

But then we recollect that, even earlier, Jean Valjean had excluded himself from the wedding party, denounced himself to Marius, and been systematically segregated from those whose felicity he could not share. Do their subsequent expressions of remorse and pleas for reintegration mean that the ending is in fact belatedly "happy" for Jean Valjean? Or should we construe his death as but another gesture of self-imposed exile, this time from life itself? Beyond earthly reconcilation and an effectual suicide, another possibility presents itself. The death of the martyred protagonist, who perceives Myriel waiting to welcome him above, may point instead to a higher form of cross-generational banquet, and hence of comic closure, namely the heavenly communion of saints.[6]

The conclusion of Hugo's novel thus lends itself to multiple interpretations, thanks to the intricate interplay of comic, tragic, and melodramatic conventions. In light of the motifs that intersect in the last four books of Part 5, the reader might entertain one additional implication as well. Considering Thénardier's shadow role as a double for Napoléon III, could not the exposure and banishment of one trickster also presage the fate of the other? The happy ending for Jean Valjean, himself a figure for the future republic, would then represent Hugo's most cherished wish for the nation itself. Rid of its phony emperor, France would at last be able to enter the blissful "afterlife" of the world that lies beyond the Second Empire.

8

Vision, Lyricism, Prophecy

The beauty of Hugo's "better world" is, however, not wholly absolute. The splendor of the future derives primarily from its contrast with the present, inglorious, state of affairs. In other words, if the here and now were not so grotesque, the then and there would not seem so sublime. The dramatic tensions that operate throughout *Les Misérables*, enhancing not only its story line but also its account of history, encompass even broader artistic concerns. For, we must remember, the novelist was among the greatest poets of his century, renowned for his prodigious output, rhetorical range, and political and cultural vision.

Above all, his primarily poetic, metaphorical view of the world must be understood as a means of exploration and discovery. Through the simultaneous clash and correlation of opposing aesthetic principles, he endeavors to apprehend and extend the limits of human perception and imagination. Antitheses give way, in Hugo's work, to a vision of the profound unity of all creation. Confrontations between the sublime and the grotesque can therefore seem as stirring as any heroic action. As the narrator declares when a potentially violent Jean Valjean stands riveted before the radiance of his slumbering host: "The moral world has no spectacle more powerful than this: a troubled, restless conscience on the verge of committing a crime, contemplating the sleep of a just man" (102). In this tableau of the grotesque pondering the sublime, the "conscience" of the felon is touched, if not yet awakened, by the revelation of Myriel's moral purity.

This scene becomes the model for other aesthetic dichotomies and resolutions. Jean Valjean beholds himself, at the moment of conversion, as a Satanic figure embraced by "the light of Paradise" (113). The virtuous Madeleine denies that he is the infamous ex-convict, but then admits to both himself and the court at Arras that they are one and the same. The digression on argot, the deformed vernacular of the underworld, bristles with elevated, poetic language. Thus, the writer's feat is to go to "the lowest depths of the social order, . . . to pursue, seize, and cast up still throbbing onto the pavement this abject idiom streaming with filth as it is dredged up into the light" (980)—a reiteration of the light-dark imagery of the earlier tableau. Opposites are reconciled in the notion that to see what is hidden in the abyss is to illuminate, and, so, to transform it.

The digression ends on a similar note: "The ideal is terrible to see, thus lost in the depths—minute, isolated, imperceptible, shining, but surrounded by all those great black menaces monstrously amassed around it, yet no more in danger than a star in the jaws of the clouds" (1002). Here, the image of looking into the abyss of social misery is also inverted, so that down becomes up as well. As with Madeleine/Jean Valjean, to fall in appearance is to rise in reality. No less "terrible" than what threatens it, the ideal can be temporarily eclipsed but never destroyed—like the eclipsed "star" (1241) of the French people itself. The monstrous grotesque inspires horror; the tiny, perfect, inviolable sublime inspires awe. Through their interaction at the very bounds of human experience, both are integral to the visionary function of Hugo's poetic prose.

To find and reveal hidden affinities is, then, an *artistic quest*, one that demands the gifts of sight and insight. In a humorous aside, the novelist alludes to his extraordinary rhetorical skills, suggesting that he is more than equal to the challenge of exploring and communicating the unknown. On the roster of bandits participating in the Gorbeau ambush, he includes himself—or a version thereof—under the alias

"Homer Hogu, a black man" (725; in French, *nègre*, which also means a ghost or hack writer). Situated between dark (a man blackened by printer's ink) and light (the dazzling poet Homer), (H)ogu/Hugo proclaims his mastery over both domains. As the inversion of his own name indicates, he mediates at the center between supposedly antithetical terms, showing each to be the reverse of the other.[1] The dramatic collisions in *Les Misérables*—between Jean Valjean and Javert, Napoléon and Wellington, parents and children, revolutionaries and conservatives, good and evil—are resolved poetically, through the interplay of opposites in metaphors and other imagery.

From this perspective, Hugo's fascination with spectacle, along with his ability to see the similar in the dissimilar, appears grounded in his celebrated visual imagination. The poetic properties of the text are not in the least subordinate to the theatrical; on the contrary, they may well predominate. The overall pattern of depicting opposing entities and bringing them into some form of harmony may be, in essence, a poetic argument. Certainly, the novel's lyrical and prophetic dimensions parallel the dialectic between self and other already observed in Jean Valjean, highlighting the themes of individual and collective identity, of self-expression and the utopian dream. In the remainder of this chapter, we will reexamine this thematic network in relation first to Hugo's lyricism and then to his visionary power.

Before the accidental drowning in 1843 of his beloved daughter Léopoldine, Hugo had published eight volumes of lyric verse that, taken together, had revolutionized the genre. After her death, he shared no poetry of the inner self—of intimate thoughts, feelings, and emotions—until the publication of *Les Contemplations* (1856). Recounting the spiritual progress of a solitary soul who seeks meaning in love and loss, life and death, suffering and expiation, the collection establishes a dialogue between the poetic *I* and the infinite. In probing the mysteries of the self, the poet at once discovers and reinforces his fundamental identity with others and, beyond, with the cosmos itself. The preface prepares the reader for this exchange in a striking formula: "People sometimes complain about writers who say *I*. . . . Alas, when I speak to you about myself, I am speaking about you. How can you not feel it? Ah, you fool, who believe that I am not you!"[2] To

Hugo's mind, some individuals who place themselves at the center of the universe may not be egocentric in the usual sense of the word. Instead, they may have entered into the cosmic economy as a vessel which has emptied itself out into everything else, and through which everything else now flows and speaks.

Similar issues emerge in *Les Misérables*, where the recurrent emphasis on the notions of selfhood and identity echoes its underlying lyricism. The endless changes of costumes and names are tied not just to dramatic art but to problems of personal authenticity and self-expression. In this context, the egoism of a Jean Valjean assumes vastly different proportions from that of a Javert or a Thénardier. To exploit others and gratify themselves, Hugo's felons project an outer semblance that has little to do with inner reality. Their identity is completely fluid because they are always "lending each other their names and their tricks, concealing themselves in their own shadow, each a refuge and a hiding place for the others, sloughing off their personalities, as one takes off a false nose at a masked ball, sometimes simplifying themselves down to one, sometimes multiplying themselves [to the point of being taken] for a mob" (724). At one level, the members of Patron-Minette enact the comradely saying, "All for one, and one for all," through a constant metamorphosis that denies any core being. At another, the dialectic between inside and outside, between the one and the many, recalls the poet's claim to speak for others when he speaks for himself.

The gangsters' status as failed artists is seen even more clearly in Thénardier. Besides his use of aliases and physical disguises, the innkeeper masks his true sentiments by glibly manipulating those of his victims, appealing to their pity, vanity, prudery, maternity, and/or humanitarian instincts—whatever is likely to trigger the desired results. Beneath the fancy speeches, the goal is to separate as many people from their money as possible, to have *all* for *him* and himself for no one. He is, in short, a hypocrite, an inauthentic voice, a counterfeit "man of letters" (378, 734). His sham compassion and superficial sentimentality—a charade of romantic sensitivity—cast him as a negative figure for Hugo himself. Through him, one might say, the poet conceals himself "in [his] own shadow" (724).

Nor is Thénardier the only "fine talker" (379) to populate the text. A host of other pontificators demonstrate the evil of empty words and false feeling: Fantine's merry but coldhearted lover Tholomyès; the self-indulgent senator from Digne, so eager to live for pleasure, and to nourish the poor with religious "myths and chimeras" (31); the pompous bourgeois in the Luxembourg Garden who lectures his child about feeding the hungry animals while the starving Magnon children watch nearby. Though law-abiding, these characters turn out to be no less egotistical, no less deceiving and self-deceived, than Hugo's criminals.

Javert's egoism is altogether different. Sacrificing all pleasures to uphold the law, he proceeds from principle alone rather than from personal reflection or desire. That he identifies fully with the legal code is evident from the beginning, since "order, law, morality, government, society itself, were personified in him, Javert" (196). He expresses society's collective will but has nothing to say on his own. The man with a "heart of wood" (193) is the creature of others, a vehicle for the convictions of the community. Thénardier spins out, for his own benefit, whatever yarns he thinks his victims want to hear. As the mouthpiece of the law, Javert never changes his tune, regardless of circumstances.

His powers of personification continue to expand when he goes to arrest Madeleine/Jean Valjean after Champmathieu's trial: "Javert was in heaven. Without a clear notion of his own feelings, yet with a confused intuition of his need and his success, he, Javert, personified justice, light, and truth, in their celestial function as destroyers of evil. He was surrounded and supported by infinite depths of authority, reason, precedent, legal conscience, the vengeance of the law, all the stars in the firmament" (290). Again we see that he speaks for society and yet lacks access to personal sentiments. The whole of nature—including the very stars in the heavens—seems implicated in the process, the fullness of the outside compensating for the emptiness of the inside. By identifying with the vast range of influences that govern him, Javert can imagine the greatness of his own sphere of influence. The fact is, however, that he can never move others because he is not inwardly moved himself.

Of course, Javert is very much moved in the end, with the revelation of Jean Valjean's sublime qualities. But while Marius responds
to the same discovery by trying to make amends, Javert commits suicide. Having abandoned his own quest to bring the outlaw to justice,
the policeman triggers a series of reflections that flesh out his psychological profile. The man with no inner life is amazed to find that he has
"under [his] breast of bronze something preposterous and disobedient
that almost resembles a heart" (1325). He has learned to understand,
to empathize with, and therefore to care about another. In conse-
quence, he has rendered good for good without any regard to external
factors. Perhaps most puzzling, he has been able "to sacrifice duty, that
general obligation, to personal motives, and to feel in these personal
motives something general too, and perhaps superior" (1320). Public
affairs have yielded to personal concerns of equal, if not greater,
weight. The dichotomy between the particular and the general has
suddenly dissolved, as private emotions have become invested with the
sense of universal value previously reserved for the legal code.

This capacity for discerning and affirming a unique identity
brings not joy and liberation but terror and disorientation: "[Javert's]
ultimate anguish was the loss of all certainty. He felt uprooted. The
code was no longer anything but a stump in his hand. . . . Within
him there was a revelation of feeling entirely distinct from the declara-
tions of the law, his only standard hitherto" (1323). Before, he was
one with the cosmos, his sentiments dictated by higher law; now he is
uprooted, sundered, set apart by internal workings as insuperable as
those of the stars. The legal machine has begun to think and feel for
himself. Even worse, he can no longer avoid thinking *about* himself.
As little as Javert is accustomed to self-scrutiny, he will have to "look
into his conscience after such shocks and render an account of himself
to himself" (1321). Self-analysis will accompany self-expression. The
trouble is that, in having to explore a whole new universe *inside*, he
knows he will never have done with the task. As Jean Valjean can
attest, "We are never done with conscience" (1387). Javert kills himself, quite simply, because he cannot deal with endlessly contemplating
his intimate connection to both the world and others, that is, with
trading his *prosaic* nature for something more *poetic*.[3]

As one might expect, the lyrical imperative of *Les Misérables* is most strongly evidenced in its heroes—Jean Valjean, Marius, the revolutionary band. The egocentric world of villainy, for example, is ironically inverted at the 1832 barricade, where those who voluntarily remain behind to die are chided by Enjolras for being "selfish" (1185). When only one need remain, five, all shouting "Me! Me! Me!" (1187), vie to attain not hedonistic gratification but the glory of self-sacrifice. As in Hugo's concept of the romantic poet, his social reformers affirm themselves through self-effacement and identification with others. It is no coincidence that one of the revolutionaries is a poet: "Jean Prouvaire . . . called himself Jehan, from that momentary little fancy that mingled with the deep and powerful movement giving rise to the study of the Middle Ages, then so necessary. [He] was addicted to love; he cultivated a pot of flowers, played the flute, wrote poetry, loved the people, pitied woman, wept over childhood, confused the future and God in the same faith" (651). His association with the great movement that had renewed interest in the Middle Ages; his love of romance, music, and nature; his compassion for all humanity; his religion of progress—such details mark him, not as just any poet, but as the romantic prototype. At once visionary and lyrical, Jean Prouvaire is a figure for Hugo himself, along with more dominant characters.

To be sure, the self-sacrificing "egoism" of the barricade defenders achieves its fullest realization in Jean Valjean. Just as the convict progresses from bearing a number for a name to assuming a long list of aliases, so he trades an acute perception of his own sufferings and grievances for sensitivity and commitment to the needs of others. Yet his self-awareness never really disappears. It is still manifest when he insists on his true identity before the court at Arras; or when he rescues Javert at the barricade with a look that says, "it is I" (1232); or when, captured at the exit to the sewers, he replies to the policeman's query, "Who are you?" by identifying himself simply as "[m]e" (1307).

At the same time, this *I* who is Jean Valjean comprises, we have seen, a large cast of alter egos. His ability to remain himself while becoming M. Madeleine, Ultime Fauchelent, and Urbain Fabre, among others, extends outward as well. Endowed with a rich empathetic imagination, he relates personally to other people regardless of age, class, or gender. He crawls under a broken wagon so that Fauchelevent can be pulled out, takes Champmathieu's place in prison, and assumes Fantine's role as mother to Cosette. He circulates in disguise throughout Paris, delivering alms to the poor. He even shows mercy to bandits, as well as to his chief antagonists, Marius and Javert. His continual self-effacement is epitomized, when, at the wedding banquet, he abandons his seat beside Cosette to Marius, and then disappears from their life entirely. Affirming himself most forcefully at the moment of greatest depersonalization, Jean Valjean corresponds to the poet as one who can ceaselessly become *other* while never losing his sense of self. In the moral and artistic universe of *Les Misérables*, egoism and selflessness coexist as complementary functions. Hugo's sublime outlaw thus represents not only Lucifer/Christ, or Napoléon, or the French nation, but the exiled author himself. He is a figure for that exceptional being called creative genius, whose self-imposed aesthetic laws resemble the autonomous rule of conscience.

Marius, too, follows a poetic trajectory, despite both his vocation as a lawyer and his apparent opposition to Jean Valjean. The biographical resonances between Marius and the novelist—alienation from republican fathers, royalist backgrounds, legal studies, virginal courtships, "wedding" nights on 16 February 1833 (in Hugo's case, with Juliette Drouet)—have not gone unnoticed.[4] But they share other similarities as well. Most notably, Marius's voice joins that of the narrator in celebrating typically lyrical subjects: nature, feminine beauty, love. In fact, one might argue, his love notes for Cosette recapitulate some of the most poetic passages in the book. The story itself is punctuated by lyrical interludes, as well as by historical digressions, but more rarely and with this difference: Hugo's use of elevated language and vivid imagery transports the reader, if only for a moment, out of the narrative and into another world altogether. Even in translation, the reader can appreciate the poetic description of the forest at night in "The Little Girl All Alone" (II.iii.5), or of love at first sight in "Effect of Spring" (III.vi.3), or of Cosette's abundantly fertile garden in "Foliis ac Frondibus" (IV.iii.3). Exalting the fecundity of her private sanctum, the writer interweaves erotic, confraternal, and cosmic imagery in a stunning tour de force.

The manuscript that Marius leaves in the garden for Cosette also occasions a poetic interlude. Yet it is important to remark that the disclosure of its contents in "A Heart Beneath a Stone" (IV.v.4) ostensibly involves a shift in voice. The "I" who speaks is the young lover himself rather than the omniscient narrator who dominates the rest of the text. The "you" addressed is not the reader but Cosette. Each brief but intensely lyrical meditation becomes a miniature prose poem, one that mirrors the poetic prose of *Les Misérables* in general. This *mise en abyme*, or reflection of the whole by the part, leads, however, to a curious effect: behind Marius, one begins to hear Hugo the poet inviting the reader to identify with the beloved. At this point, Marius's character evokes the author perhaps less as young lover than as young poetic genius.

In any event, the notebook again underscores how closely self and world, lyrical and visionary modes, are related in *Les Misérables*. Through metaphorical language, which forges analogies between disparate entities, it intertwines the private thoughts, emotions, and experiences of those who love with the workings of the entire universe. The connection is established in the very first sentence—"The reduction of the universe to a single being, the expansion of a single being into God, this is love" (932)—and restated again and again over the next three and a half pages, though never in the same words. Echoing Pascal's *Pensées* (1670), Marius's reflections plumb the mysteries that bind "the infinitely great and the infinitely small" (933) in one great cosmic dance. Each a variation on the theme of love's tranformational power, his ideas germinate as profusely as the vegetation in Cosette's garden. The prodigality of God's creation is emulated by the fruitfulness of the inspired lover/poet.

But inspiration can run both ways. The small can enkindle the great, since "If no one loved, the sun would go out" (935). The apocalyptic undertone of this, Marius's final message to Cosette, demonstrates the proximity for the novelist of prophecy and lyricism, vision and insight. The tiny pinpoints of eye, soul, and heart can expand both inward and outward to touch all that is—and all that might be. "The future belongs still more to the heart than the mind," the young man writes. "To love is the only thing that can occupy and fill up eternity.

The infinite requires the inexhaustible" (932). Marius's potential as a visionary, concerned like his revolutionary friends with the future of the French nation, seems assured by his passionate focus on the eternal and the infinite. Capable of transcending space and time through the imagination, he may even be able to escape the trap of middle-class mentality poised to close over him at the end.

Indeed, references abound to Marius's visionary capacity, references that affiliate him with such "seers" as Myriel, Jean Valjean, Enjolras, and Hugo himself. To grasp the significance of this trait in the young hero, we should first examine how it functions elsewhere in the text. For although the story line does not begin gaining momentum until Jean Valjean's encounter with the bishop in Book 2 ("The Fall"), the potency of vision per se is stressed from the outset. Myriel's habit of meditating in his garden, we learn, reveals many of nature's secrets. With "the eye of a linguist deciphering a palimpsest" (53), he foreshadows Marius in pondering the wonders of creation, from the sublime to the grotesque, from the infinitely great to the infinitely small. He is moved rather than disturbed by "monstrosities" (53) of appearance or behavior. As a result, he does not judge but interrogates "the portion of chaos" still left in nature, "thoughtfully seeking, beyond apparent life, for its cause, its explanation, or its excuse" (53). A certain amount of disorder is normal, if not necessary, in the larger scheme of things. As his gaze shifts from tiny deformities to "the visible splendors of the constellations and the invisible splendor of God" (55), the scope of his wisdom seems to expand immeasurably as well. He penetrates each layer of the divine "palimpsest" as an act of reverence.

Such discernment, Hugo insists, does not require superhuman powers. The wonders of the universe await all who can open their eyes to see them. In this regard, Myriel serves as a both a comforter and a guide to the bereaved, encouraging them to view the world anew. "Look steadfastly and you will see the living glory of your beloved dead in the heights of heaven" (17), he invites. Instead of fixating on "the grave," that is, on the grotesque, they should "loo[k] up to the stars" (17), that is, to the sublime. This ability to "read" what lies in darkness not only illustrates the romantic/idealist notion of a higher reality beyond the range of the senses. It also implicitly counters the positivist materialism of the senator from Digne, who claims to be certain about the finality of death. "Let us look for the real, down deep, right to the bottom. We should sniff out the truth, dig underground, and grab it" (30), he declares, his rooting around in the dirt like a pig after truffles contrasting with Myriel's upward gaze. One discovers, Hugo suggests, what one seeks. To look no farther than the end of one's nose for something to believe in is, in effect, to "confuse heaven's radiant stars with a duck's footprint left in the mud" (52). And to trust the judgment of anyone who does so is dangerous folly.

At first glance, the reader might consider these developments to favor a religious viewpoint. Yet at the close of Book 2, Hugo carefully distances himself from Myriel. The good priest, he remarks, has his limitations, since he does not attempt to pierce the "difficult problems, sinister depths" (58) of existence—good and evil, destiny, nature, the soul, aggression, conscience, the transformation by death, being and nothingness, freedom and necessity. In lacking the will and the imagination alike to probe all these "unfathomable . . . profundities" (57), Myriel can only gesture toward the spiritual adventures of the visionary poet. Most so-called wisdom sees glory in the commonplace, stars in muddy duckprints. The bishop, on the other hand, sees one kind of glory in another, the stars as signs of the imperishable soul. But, for Hugo, genius actually *creates* glory: it contemplates the heavens with "that flaming eye that seems, looking steadfastly into the infinite, to kindle the very stars" (58). In finding hidden realities and bringing them to light, the poet continually charts new territory. As we have noted, this drive to expand the known universe also characterizes Marius's reflections on love, Jean Valjean's quest for spiritual progress, and the forward march of history. The reader can therefore anticipate that, through his visionary talents, Marius will be inextricably connected both to the ex-convict and to French utopian thought.

Thus, beyond their obvious dissimilarities, the novel's two protagonists have in common not just their love for Cosette but the poetic gift of sight. In the case of Jean Valjean, this faculty carries him into a whole new realm of being quite early in the text. We are reminded during his conversion experience, for instance, that "Excessive misfor-

tune . . . had made him somehow a visionary" (112). Now he apprehends his self-centered wretchedness so distinctly in the light of
Myriel's benevolence that the image of his ominous soul is projected
outward, passing before his eyes like a hallucination. The possibility of
going mad is very real. "His brain was in one of those violent, yet
frighteningly calm, states where reverie is so profound it swallows up
reality," Hugo explains. "We no longer see the objects before us, but
we see, as if outside of ourselves, the forms we have in our minds"
(112). Having been intimately acquainted with mental illness—both
his brother Eugène and daughter Adèle were victims of severe psy-
choses—the writer is keenly aware of the fine line that divides inspiration from dementia.[5]

At first it is difficult to guess how Jean Valjean will emerge from
his hallucinatory state. Described as a "kind of ecstasy" (113), his revelation breaks down the boundaries between dream and reality, inside
and outside, self and other. Just as reality vanishes in the face of reverie, so does the bishop's image expand to engulf him, filling his soul
"with a magnificent radiance" (113). The danger is that, as an individ-
ually constituted self, he will disappear forever. Yet the hero's sense of
self immediately returns, no longer diminished through humility but
expanded through the birth of conscience. Reality is not, in the end,
denied; it is transformed by the dreamer's visionary power into a higher truth. Likewise, in the mental tempest provoked by the
Champmathieu affair, he sees his duty "written in luminous letters flar-
ing out before his eyes and moving with his gaze: '*Go! Give thy name!
Denounce thyself!*'" (228). Inner moral dictates are projected onto the
outer world, spelling out his subsequent decision. When we later learn
that, as a gardener in the Petit-Picpus convent, Jean Valjean "would
lean on his spade and descend slowly along the endless spirals of reverie" (569), we recognize his bent for active, probing meditation.

Two other crises confirm Jean Valjean's uncommon visual acu-
ity: the chase through Paris and the barricade scene. Each episode
involves fleeing from a death trap with a younger, helpless person
whose life depends upon him. When Javert, accompanied by other
police agents, corners him at night in an unknown part of the urban
landscape, the convict is at a loss to save himself and Cosette. How

does one escape with a child from a dead end? The answer lies in a tiny detail of his surroundings: "All extreme situations have their flashes that sometimes blind us, sometimes illuminate us. Jean Valjean's desperate gaze encounterd the lamppost in the Cul-de-sac Genrot" (458). In short, he has a stroke of genius. A rope cut, a wall scaled, and the two fugitives find refuge at the convent.

A decade later he finds himself similarly trapped with Marius as the government troops close in on the barricade. Having retreated to a sheltered recess behind a corner of the Corinth tavern, he must find a way *out* before the others get *in*. Once again, he casts his eyes about, seeking the impossible. Once again, the impossible materializes from out of nowhere: "Jean Valjean looked at the house in front of him, he looked at the barricade beside him, then he looked at the ground, with the violence of last extremity, in desperation, as if he wanted to bore a hole in it with his eyes. Because of his persistent stare, something vaguely tangible . . . outlined itself and took shape at his feet, as if there were a power in the eye to make the desired thing appear" (1254–55). An escape route hatches beneath his piercing eye, this time in the form of a removable sewer grating. For the visionary outlaw, as for the person of faith, to seek is to find. Imagination opens up new realities.

The spiritual dimensions of seeing are again evident as he somehow manages to make his way in the pitch-black sewer itself, like "the creatures of the night groping in the invisible, and lost underground in the veins of darkness" (1278). Not only must one navigate blindly in such conditions. Sight itself does not mean salvation, since there are no signposts for the exit from this nightmarish, Dantesque underworld. In the hero's case, however, some measure of vision returns. "The pupil dilates in the night, and at last finds day in it," the narrator insists, "even as the soul dilates in misfortune, and at last finds God in it" (1278–79). To invent a moral self is to scrutinize and decipher the unknown. Resembling the "expansion of a single being into God" (932) that Marius defines in his notebook as love, seeing *is* believing for Jean Valjean—and vice versa.

From this perspective, the transcendent connotations of the outlaw's burial in the Vaugirard cemetery, as in his ordeal in the sewer, are inscribed in imagery of sight. In an electrifying moment, after Fauchelevent pries open the lid of the coffin, he thrills to the discovery that "Jean Valjean's eyes were open, and gazing at him" (560). The double promise of resurrection inherent in these two scenes is fulfilled in the dénouement. As he lies dying, Jean Valjean sees the bishop in the shadows, a sign that he will escape with his life from death itself. The "light of the unknown world . . . already visible in his eye" (1460) indicates that, right to the end, he acts as a kind of poetic intermediary, shedding light for others on what they cannot yet perceive.

Present with Cosette at the hero's deathbed, Marius is clearly implicated in this transference, the genealogy of which goes back to the beginning of the text. In "The Bishop in the Presence of an Unfamiliar Light" (I.i.10), Myriel is moved during his visit with the dying Revolutionary G. by "the reflection of that great conscience upon his own" (45). The bishop in turn transforms Jean Valjean through unexpected generosity. After the convict robs Petit Gervais, he suddenly views his whole life in "a light he had never seen before" (113)—again the illumination of one conscience by another. Logically, then, the strange light that Marius glimpses in the dying man's eyes should have a similar effect him and, in the event, on the next generation.

Numerous passages devoted to Marius's own visionary potential confirm the complex correlation between these two characters. First, Jean Valjean's conversion by Myriel prefigures the moment when the French Revolution and the First Empire fall into "luminous perspective before [Marius's] straining eyes" (631; in French, *devant sa prunelle visionnaire*, literally, before his visionary pupil[s]), revealing their true splendor. The imagery of obscurity that accompanies the exconvict's meditations reappears in regard to the budding royalist who, as he later puts it, has had a "cataract" (687) removed. But, as with Jean Valjean, Marius's evolution is not completed in a day. The narrator quickly adds: "We are describing the state of a mind on the march. Progress is not accomplished at a bound" (631). Like the hero, or history itself, Marius's "mind on the march" may take a wrong turn from time to time; its advance remains ineluctable.

The young man's subsequent leaps forward occur in conjunction with other vivid perceptions, many of which are again related to sight.

Through the ordeal of poverty, the plight of society's outcasts—of such *misérables* as Fantine, Jean Valjean, Eponine, the utopian revolutionaries—becomes part of Marius's permanent identity. To earn his living as a translator, he, too, must bear the cold, the dark, the despair. These conditions, delineated in "The Excellence of Misfortune" (III.v), serve as a sorting factor by which people become either "infamous" or "sublime" (678), Thénardiers or Jean Valjeans. The material world can affect one's spiritual welfare because, Marius realizes, "all extremes meet" (682). His moral discernment thus has a poetic corollary: the "romantic" ability to discover resemblances beneath apparent differences. At the same time, destitution brings disdain for the material, coupled with "yearnings toward the ideal life" (685). Poverty stimulates his imagination to dream of a better world.

In this better world he is not alone. Marius's solitary reflections enable him to move from the particular to the general, from his own situation to that of humankind: "From the egotism of the suffering man, he passes to the compassion of the contemplating man" (685). His own adversity opens his eyes to the misery of others. The lyricism of his notes for Cosette is inseparable from sensitivity to others. He whose "eyes were small, their outlook vast" (699) seems destined for collective, utopian matters. A "millionaire of intelligence," Marius reproduces Jean Valjean's universal empathy—"forgetfulness of self, and pity for all" (685)—through a richly populated imagination. So, too, his extensive sympathies preempt any political partisanship, despite his friendship with the republican revolutionaries. Like the outlaw, he belongs only to the "party of humanity" (693). At times, however, his disinterestedness resembles not so much political apathy as artistic detachment. Consider the scene where he watches Thénardier prepare to ambush Jean Valjean. When moonlight floods the villain's lair, "to Marius's poetic mind, a dreamer even in the moment of action, it was like a thought of heaven mingled with the misshapen nightmares of earth" (782). Perceiving the sublime in the midst of the grotesque, the young man transcends the dystopian present through the creative imagination. Where "extremes meet" (682) visions of harmony are born.

Still, Marius's dreams do not lead him to the systematic charity of Madeleine in Montreuil-sur-mer or of the fugitive hero in Paris. His "[p]rogress" (631), in fact, has not yet resulted in any substantial action of any sort. To the contrary, "he sometimes spent whole days like a visionary, thinking, deep in the mute joys of contemplation and inner radiance" (686). Feeding on reverie while he pines for Cosette, he enters a phase where he risks something worse than starvation. The drowning imagery associated elsewhere with Jean Valjean, Javert, and *les misérables* in general reappears in the caveat that too much dreaming "submerges and drowns" (861) the dreamer. According to the narrator, this "fatal slope" leads inexorably to a hole, to "suicide or crime" (862), to Thénardier's hovel of evil or Javert's watery grave. Marius runs a double moral jeopardy through material deprivation and excessive daydreaming.

To counter this slippery slope, just as Jean Valjean defeats his personal inclinations, some form of social commitment is necessary. Realigning the inner self must result in exterior activity. If it is true that "Each of us dreams the unknown and the impossible according to his own nature" (693), then generous dreams must be translated—as Marius's temporary profession implies—into charitable deeds. The text says categorically that he will not be long in turning his reveries into initiatives: "It was clear that, for his energetic and generous nature, this could only be a transitory state, and that at the first shock against the inevitable complications of destiny, Marius would awaken" (686). The defense of the barricade, the death of all his friends, a wealthily endowed love match, the revelations of Jean Valjean and Thénardier—one would think these sufficient "shocks" to jolt him out of his lethargy.

We might therefore be surprised that Hugo's fourth-generation "visionary" does not spring into action before the end of the novel. G. dies in 1815, the same year as Napoléon's defeat; Myriel, in 1821; Enjolras and his entire band of revolutionary idealists, in June 1832; Jean Valjean, in June 1833.[6] Marius alone remains to carry social change forward into the future. So where exactly does he stand at the dénouement? We know that, although a "democrat," the newly married Baron Pontmercy cannot refrain from judging the confessed ex-convict several months earlier. "He had not yet . . . adopted all the ideas of progress" (1411), the narrator explains once again. He automatically accepts the workings of the penal system; social damnation is not to be questioned. Unlike Myriel, he cannot apprehend the place of the grotesque, of disorder, in the overall cosmic design. But a qualification, now reiterated for the third time, immediately follows: "He was still at that point, though he was to advance infallibly with time, his nature being good, and basically composed entirely of latent progress" (1411). This promise, so congruent with Marius's visionary gifts, suggests that he will, eventually, become Jean Valjean's spiritual heir. Their thematic *affiliation* can be read as a kind of verbal play on the notion of a son, or *fils*. Having already inherited both Cosette and, through her, Jean Valjean's material fortune, Marius is in a position to take up the cause of social justice as well. Discovering his own father's valor opened the way to political conversion.[7] His adoptive father's even more difficult heroism should produce an analogous transformation.

To do so will first require the revelation of the outlaw's lofty virtue as the progressive reformer Madeleine, as Javert's rescuer at the barricade, and as his own silent savior—a revelation that does not occur until just before the closing deathbed scene. Marius thus learns several crucial lessons all at once: that he has been an "unnatural ingrate" (1452), returning cold rejection for the other's self-sacrifice; that his actions have doubtless hastened Jean Valjean's tragic death; and, most significantly, that even the most wretched members of society have enormous potential. What the young lawyer has not yet realized is that, with only a slight shift in circumstances, he too could have ended up at the other end of the legal system. Poverty may have failed to turn him into a Thénardier, but his presence on the republican barricades could well have resulted in prison or summary execution. Instead, he has been able to enjoy love and prosperity, unconcerned about being prosecuted for his part in the 1832 insurrection. He is free today, beside Cosette, because of sacrifices made yesterday by his friends, by Javert, and by Jean Valjean—not to mention those made even earlier by the revolutionaries of 1789, by his own father, and by Fantine, whose name the hero discloses just before he dies.

Vision, Lyricism, Prophecy

When we read the last page of *Les Misérables*, then, with its description of Jean Valjean's neglected grave and final anonymity, are we to believe that Marius has squandered his spiritual inheritance, that he has lost or denied his capacity for envisioning alternative worlds? Has he renounced his intention, declared to Cosette, to "spend the rest of [his] life in venerating [Jean Valjean]" (1452)? Although critics have often assumed this pessimistic stance, let us not forget that the grave is precisely as Jean Valjean wanted it. His dying request—"you will have me buried in the most convenient plot of ground under a stone to mark the spot. That is my wish. No name on the stone" (1460)—has therefore been granted. In this context, the open-ended conclusion can be interpreted as forecasting not Marius's indifference to the dead but the devotion of his energies to the living. Only Jean Valjean's physical remains are to be found in the cemetery; his saintly soul, we are given to understand, resides in bliss, where it will welcome, like Myriel, the next generation of generous individuals.

Meanwhile, the have-nots—the poor, the uneducated, the unloved—need the devoted attention of the haves. Whether the convict's higher conscience passes to Marius is, in the last analysis, less important than whether it passes to Hugo's bourgeois reader. The young man's evolution—that metamorphosis "in gradual phases" which is "the case with many minds of our time" (630)—implicates us as well. Blessed with relative prosperity, we are all challenged by the text to "drea[m] the unknown and the impossible" (693), to harness to social action our vision of a better world.

And just what, according to Hugo, might this world look like? The visionary qualities of dreaming and contemplation, as enacted through Myriel, Jean Valjean, and Marius, find perhaps their highest expression in Enjolras. To fill in the details about the shape of the utopian future, the novelist enlists the combined voices of the "Friends of the ABC," with the revolutionary leader's foremost among them. Thus, when Enjolras plans a speech that will rally others to the republican cause, he draws on their collective strengths: "He was inwardly composing, with the philosophical and penetrating eloquence of Combeferre, the cosmopolitan enthusiasm of Feuilly, Courfeyrac's animation, Bahorel's laughter, Jean Prouvaire's melancholy, Joly's science, and Bossuet's sarcasms, a sort of electric spark to catch fire in all directions at once. All of them put to work" (857). He is, in every sense, their spokesperson. This ability to synthesize a wide range of viewpoints and rhetorical styles points, of course, to Hugo himself. But it also anticipates Enjolras's fiery oration, in "What Horizon Is Visible from the Top of the Barricade" (V.i.v), in the face of impending death. Here, as in the scene where the rebel chief executes the police spy Le Cabuc, Hugo recapitulates the essence of liberal republican thought.[8]

The world for which the revolutionaries are prepared to die presents itself as a vision of universal peace and harmony, firmly grounded in the principles of liberty, equality, and fraternity. As Enjolras declares:

> Citizens, do you imagine the future? The streets of the cities flooded with light, green branches on the thresholds, the nations sisters, men just, the old blessing the children, the past loving the present, thinkers in full liberty, believers in full equality[;] . . . to all, labor; for all, law; over all, peace. . . . [Equality] is all aptitudes having equal opportunity; politically, all votes having equal weight; religiously, all consciences having equal rights. Equality has an organ: free and compulsory education. The right to the alphabet, we must begin by that. . . . Yes, education! Light! Light! Everything comes from light, and everything returns to it. Citizens, the nineteenth century is great, but the twentieth century will be happy. . . . The human race will fulfill its law as the terrestrial globe fulfills its own; harmony will be re-established between the soul and the star; the soul will gravitate about the truth like the star about the light. . . . Brothers, whoever dies here dies in the radiance of the future, and we are entering a grave illuminated by the dawn. (1189–91)

Without reproducing his entire speech, we can catch the drift of Enjolras's program for social reform: international peace; universal suffrage; the right to work; equal opportunity; universal education; penal reform; technological progress; freedom of thought, religion, and the press. In other words, he reiterates in 1832 many of the goals of the Revolution of 1789—goals that had been recycled in the July Revolution of 1830 and that would again impel the February

Revolution of 1848. In a way, he not only foresees their initial implementation in 1848 under a republican socialist government; he also recognizes Hugo's efforts to pursue them after the conservative backlash, during his three years as an elected representative to the Legislative Assembly. The insurgents' ideal future consists in at last fulfilling these same objectives.

Recalling other "visionary" passages in *Les Misérables*, the emphasis on light in Enjolras's speech again links reading—the "right to the alphabet" (1190)—with the ability to see beyond one's personal interests. His utopianism thus repeats the intertwining of self and cosmos in, for example, Marius's notebook, or Myriel's garden, or Jean Valjean's luminous death scene. In the future, harmony will prevail between people and nations on the one hand and between society and the natural order on the other. But the notion that progress is as ineluctable as the laws that govern the universe has other ramifications as well. To predict the reestablishment of cosmic harmony is to intimate that the cause of its disruption will be removed.

Through Enjolras, then, Hugo unleashes his own prophetic powers regarding the world to come *after* the Second Empire. He *reads* the future as *other*. He alludes to these powers—and to their consequences—in a reference to Saint John the Divine: "We do not speak of the sublime exile of Patmos, who also bears down on the real world with a protest in the name of the ideal, makes a tremendous satire of a vision, and throws on Nineveh-Rome, on Babylon-Rome, on Sodom-Rome, the flaming reverberations of the Apocalypse" (1052). A model for the exiled Hugo, the author of the Book of Revelations likewise allies satire with prophecy. The apocalyptic end of Nineveh, Babylon, and Sodom—punished for their wickedness—is but another way of foreseeing the fall of Rome. And, we may remember, Rome is, in Hugo's system, but a symbol of the present. Just as the poet's shadow history of the Second Empire implies a political ideal, Enjolras's vision on the barricades, purportedly aimed at the July Monarchy, indicts Napoléon III's reign. When Hugo therefore parades the various ancient civilizations that have vanished from the earth—"India, Chaldea, Persia, Assyria, Egypt, . . . Babylon, Nineveh, Tarsus, Thebes, Rome" (1001)—he is also bringing a mighty curse to bear against the current regime. Like the prophets of old, he dooms self-centered decadence to the wrath of God and the dustbin of history.

Throughout the novel, Hugo offers additional glimpses into his reading of the utopian future. In "A Parenthesis" (II.vii), he anticipates Enjolras's embrace of universal instruction when he extols the benefits of wisdom and learning: "To offer thought to men's thirst, to give everyone, as an elixir, the idea of God, to make conscience and science fraternize in them, and to make them good men by this mysterious confrontation—such is the province of true philosophy" (519). Taking up G.'s claim that "Conscience is science" (39), he suggests that education will put end to crime by awakening moral understanding.

The theme recurs in "Paris Atomized" (III.i), where he proposes a cure for that symptom of social illness, the street urchin. The nation cries out for a new version of the Enlightenment: "All the generous sunrays of society spring from science, letters, the arts, and education. . . . Give [young people] light, so they can give you warmth. Sooner or later, the splendid question of universal education will take its position with the irresistible authority of absolute truth; and then those who govern . . . will have to make this choice: the children of France or the *gamins* of Paris; flames in the light or will o' the wisps in the gloom" (587–88). Once more, learning appears as the key to generosity, to giving warmth, to caring about others. The compelling power of truth, like the laws of the universe, will finally drive society to create not illiterate, poverty-striken nonentities but citizens of France. "Destroy the cave Ignorance, and you destroy the mole Crime" (721), he maintains in his discussion of argot. An enlightened populace will spawn a productive workforce, rather than agents of social destruction.

In "A Few Pages of History" (IV.i), Hugo continues to trace this view of *future history*, under the guise of outlining the socialist agenda of the early 1830s. Like Enjolras, he believes that human happiness will prevail when the "rights" (840) of all people—including women and children—are finally respected. To leave some to misery is to harm the entire social body. "[L]earn to produce wealth and learn to distribute it, and you will have material grandeur and moral grandeur combined; and you shall be worthy of calling yourselves France" (842), he

concludes, indicating that true progress will begin with the rehabilitation of democratic republican aims.

This appeal to the higher nature of his compatriots reechoes in
his praise of self-sacrifice in "The Dead Are Right and the Living Are
Not Wrong" (V.i.20), as well as in the digression on the sewers. The
theme of hunger that pervades the novel—and that underlies the
image of the city's digestive tract—provides an opportunity for imag-
ining a more glorious future. The visionary poet can look at filth and
see in it prosperity for all. In a striking metaphor he declares, "If our
gold is manure, on the other hand, our manure is gold" (1256). By
failing to recycle its detritus, France throws a fortune away every year.
All this slime, he imagines, is "the flowering meadow, it is the green
grass, it is marjoram and thyme and sage, it is game, it is cattle, it is the
satisfied lowing of huge oxen in the evening, it is perfumed hay, it is
golden wheat, it is bread on your table, it is warm blood in your veins,
it is health, it is joy, it is life" (1257). In yet another metaphorical
development, set in the present tense, he makes the miracle happen in
the here and now. If we can envision it, we can set about realizing it
for tomorrow.

But the metaphor extends even further: his praise of sewage
recalls his repetition of Cicero's remark, *"Fex urbis, [lex orbis]"* (593,
1170; Dregs [or excrement] of the city, law of the world), in reflecting
on the potential of *les misérables*. The world will be shaped, one way
or another, by the masses. As indicated by the chapter title, "The
Future Latent in the People" (III.i.12), tomorrow depends on fostering
the potential of all citizens today. To reveal through contemplation the
"nether magnificences" (1170) of sewers or rabble is to strike gold on
behalf of the entire nation.

While the absence of any detailed social program might seem
puzzling, it is important to note the enormous drawbacks of including
one. In the first place, it is it is much easier to find flaws in a comprehensive plan for utopia than in irony or satire. Conversely, it is less difficult to criticize the worst aspects of something that already exists
than to construct something new. Political programs are, at best, time-
ly. But in works of art, which aspire to be timeless, they are always
dated. Any attempt at specifics would therefore have undermined the

novel's story line, as well as its satirical qualities, by drawing too much attention to highly debatable issues. Instead, Hugo creates a remarkable consistency of tone, imagery, and outlook by continually focusing on the larger picture. It is no accident that he so often gestures toward the cosmos as an image of the sublime. As the genius who contemplates the heavens with "that flaming eye that seems . . . to kindle the very stars" (58), the visionary poet strives above all to touch the divine and, thereby, to point the right way to the future.[9]

The suggestive power of *Les Misérables* is thus intimately related to Hugo's refusal to develop any systematic ideological construct. His aim is higher: to illuminate the whole of reality by infusing realism with the imaginary, what *is* with a sense of what *might be*. The resulting *irrealism*, as one might call it, engages the reader in an adventure of rediscovery. To this end, Hugo deconstructs realist conventions at various levels of the text: in the unexplained ruptures in Jean Valjean's biography, the discontinuities and fragmentations of character, the digressive interruptions of the plot, and the constant shift of registers and genres.

The hero's visionary traits demonstrate the shifting ground of "the real" in a number of ways as well. Not only can he perceive what is not visible—the bishop's radiant image, the eye of God upon him, a means of escape from a dead-end street or the barricades or the sewers, the beckoning light of the afterlife. Under stressful circumstances, he can also transform what he sees. Such heightened creativity is evidenced in the sudden hallucinatory appearance of the familiar and the commonplace. The hinge on the bishop's door creaks loudly as the intruder enters, "barking like a dog to waken all sleepers" (100); Petit Gervais's stolen coin is "an open eye staring at him" (108); the polished brass door handle to the courtroom at Arras shines for him "like an ominous star . . . [or] the eye of a tiger" (264); the ray of light that he notices through the keyhole of his hideaway in the Gorbeau tenement is "an evil star in the black background of the door and the wall" (443). Similarly the reversed words on Cosette's blotter "produced the effect on him of an apparition in a flash of lightning. It was a hallucination. It was impossible. It could not be" (1152). That reality becomes *other* for Jean Valjean, appearing to scrutinize *him*, is the corollary of his ability to project, to invent, new realities. The isolation and dismantling of everyday objects likewise enable the reader to peer into the depths of the "ordinary" and so to discern its hidden, extraordinary possibilities.[10]   In each case, the text stimulates our awareness that nothing can be taken for granted, that everything has multiple as-yet-unknown sides.

The sublime is all around us, if only we can learn to see it. Hugo challenges the reader to *realize*—both to apprehend and to create—the wonders of the utopian world to come.

9

Epilogue: The One and the Many

Les Misérables is a work to which one can return time and again without a sense of having exhausted its possibilities. Like its multifaceted hero, it can be viewed from numerous perspectives, each enriching the others. It is tragedy, comedy, melodrama, romance, satire, epic, poetry, history, philosophy, theology, and political polemic, all rolled into one. It enables us to escape into the adventures of others; it brings us back to ourselves. It is a one-of-a-kind book that tries to say just about everything while yet leaving a great deal to the reader's own imagination.

Add to this the many stage and screen adaptations—at least three new film versions were scheduled for 1995 alone—and the occasions for discovering still *other* voices, for seeing still *other* sides, can only multiply. The expanding horizon envisoned by Enjolras on the barricade is, finally, that of Hugo's boundless novel itself.

Notes and References

Chapter 1. Hugo's Times

1. Victor Hugo, *Les Misérables*, trans. Lee Fahnestock and Norman Macafee, based on Charles E. Wilbour's translation (New York: New American Library [Signet Classic], 1987), 1; hereafter cited in text.

2. I adhere to the standard mode of designating section titles in *Les Misérables*, the parenthetical numbers indicating, respectively, the Part, Book, and Chapter of the text.

Chapter 2. Importance of the Work

1. France Vernier, *"Les Misérables* ou: De la modernité," *Hugo le fabuleux*, Actes du Colloque de Cerisy, 30 June–10 July, 1985, eds. Jacques Seebacher and Anne Ubersfeld (Paris: Seghers, 1985), 67–69; hereafter cited in text.

Chapter 3. Critical Reception

1. Pierre Malandain, "La réception des *Misérables* ou Un lieu où des convictions sont en train de se former,'" *Revue d'histoire littéraire de la France* 86, no. 6 (November–December 1986): 1065; hereafter cited in text.

2. Max Bach, "Critique et politique: la réception des *Misérables* en 1862," *PMLA* 77, no. 5 (December 1962): 596–99; hereafter cited in text.

3. Charles-Augustin Sainte-Beuve, *Mes Poisons* (Paris: Editions Plasma, 1980), 61.

4. Claude Gély, *Hugo et sa fortune littéraire* (Bordeaux: Guy Ducros, 1970), 58.

5. George Sand, *La Revue des deux mondes* (n.d.), quoted in Claude Gély, *Hugo*, 90; Arthur Rimbaud, letter to Paul Demeny, *Oeuvres complètes*, eds. Rolland de Renéville and Jules Mouquet (Paris: Gallimard, 1954), 272; Émile Zola, *Oeuvres complètes*, ed. Henri Mitterand, 15 vols. (Paris: Cercle du Livre Précieux, 1966–70), 12:148.

6. Marie-Sophie Armstrong, "Hugo's 'égouts' and *Le ventre de Paris*," *French Review* 69, no. 3 (February 1996), 394–408, and "Une lecture 'Hugo-centrique' de *La Fortune des Rougons*," *Romanic Review* (forthcoming) have established a wide range of Hugolian echoes in Zola. See also Auguste Dezalay, "Lecture du génie. Génie de la lecture: *Germinal* et *Les Misérables*," *Revue d'histoire littéraire de la France* 3 (1985): 435–46.

7. Philippe Chardin, "Dostoïevski lecteur de V. Hugo," *Le Rayonnement international de Victor Hugo*, ed. Francis Claudon, Proceedings of the International Comparative Literature Association, 11th international congress, Paris, August 1985 (New York: Peter Lang, 1989), 160, 164, and 168. And Victor Brombert, *Victor Hugo and the Visionary Novel* (Cambridge: Harvard University Press, 1984), 2; hereafter cited in text.

8. Michel Cadot, "Leon Tolstoï lecteur et traducteur de Victor Hugo," *Le Rayonnement international de Victor Hugo*, 170, 172, and 174.

9. Naoki Inagaki, "Les Traductions de Victor Hugo en japonais," *Le Rayonnement international de Victor Hugo*, 264–65.

10. Jean Cocteau, "Le Mystère laïc," *Oeuvres complètes*, vol. 10 (Lausanne: Editions Marguerat, 1950), 21. See Pierre Albouy, "La Vie posthume de Victor Hugo," in *Oeuvres complètes* of Victor Hugo, ed. Jean Massin, 18 vols. (Paris: Le Club Français du Livre, 1967–70), 16:xxv; and Pascale Devars, Edgar Petitier, Guy Rosa, and Alain Vaillant, "Si Victor Hugo était compté," in *Gloire de Victor Hugo*, Ministère de Culture (Paris Editions de la Réunion des Musées Nationaux, 1985), 359–60; hereafter cited in text.

11. André Malraux, *Anti-mémoires* (Paris: Gallimard, 1972), 198–99. Perhaps not coincidentally, Victor Hugo is numbered among the saints of the Cao Dai sect, one of Vietnam's exotic blends of religions.

12. Madeleine Rebérioux and Maurice Agulhon, "Hugo dans le débat politique et social," in *Gloire de VH*, 230 and 234–35; hereafter cited in text. Let us also note that Georges Ascoli, the first professor to hold the Hugo chair at the Sorbonne, died at Auschwitz in 1944 (Albouy, "La Vie posthume," xxiv).

13. Louis Aragon, *Avez-vous lu Victor Hugo?* (Paris: Editeurs Français Réunis, 1952), 41 and 8.

14. I am grateful to Penguin Books Ltd., London, for their generous assistance with recent sales and publication figures, as furnished on 8 September 1994.

Chapter 4. Romance and the Sublime Outlaw

1. Richard B. Grant treats the relationship between *Les Misérables*, *La Fin de Satan*, and *La Légende des siècles* in *The Perilous Quest: Image, Myth,*

and Prophecy in the Narratives of Victor Hugo (Durham: Duke University Press, 1968), 155–60, 168, and 173–76; hereafter cited in text.

2. See my analysis in *The Early Novels of Victor Hugo: Towards a Poetics of Harmony* (Geneva: Droz, 1986), 165–70, 181–86, and 189–91.

3. George Piroué, *Victor Hugo romancier ou les dessus de l'inconnu* (Paris: Denoël, 1964), 50, views Jean Valjean as a "man of tomorrow, [who] agrees to spend a lifetime bringing forth his conversion."

4. Madeleine's dream before setting out for Arras can be read, then, as representing the nightmarish aspects of losing another self, the "brother of whom . . . I never think and whom I scarcely remember" (237). See Anne Ubersfeld's psychoanalytic interpretation of the dream in *Paroles de Hugo* (Paris: Messidor, 1985), 117–31.

5. For the poetry on children and family life, see especially *Les Feuilles d'automne* (1831), *Les Contemplations* (1856), and *L'Art d'être grand-père* (1877).

6. Nicole Savy offers a provocative analysis of the significance and limitations of Cosette's character in "Cosette: un personnage qui n'existe pas," *Lire* Les Misérables, eds. Anne Ubersfeld and Guy Rosa (Paris: José Corti, 1985), 173–90.

Chapter 5. Historical Perpectives

1. Entitled *Jean Tréjean* when Hugo began writing in 1845, the novel was at first more concerned with the outlaw's own story than with its historical and social context. But by the end of 1847, the author had signed a contract for a book called *Les Misères,* the focus having already shifted toward a much broader account of suffering humanity.

2. For a highly useful outline and discussion of the chronology in the text from the birth in 1729 of the Revolutionary G. to Jean Valjean's death in 1833, see Yves Gohin, "Une histoire qui date," in *Lire* Les Misérables, 29–57.

3. I deal with the existential aspects of the correspondence between hero and nation in "Jean Valjean and France: Outlaws in Search of Integrity," *Stanford French Review* 2, no. 3 (Winter 1978): 363–74.

Chapter 6. Back to the Future

1. Victor Hugo, *Actes et Paroles* I, *Avant l'exil,* in *Oeuvres,* 7:220.

2. See my discussion of these two works in *Early Novels,* 62–102 and 111—58, respectively.

3. It is essential to note that, in 1848, liberal republicans—the proponents of popular democracy—subscribed to "utopian socialist" thinking in the French pre-Marxist, humanitarian, Fourierist/Saint-Simonian tradition, as opposed to the "scientific socialism" of Marx and Engels.

4. As Hugo had declared in 1848 to the poet-politician Alphonse de Lamartine, "The Republic is, in my opinion, the only rational government, the only one worthy of nations. The universal Republic will be the last word of progress" (*Oeuvres*, 7:1080).

5. See Northrop Frye, *Anatomy of Criticism: Four Essays* (Princeton: Princeton University Press, 1957): "Satire demands at least a token fantasy, a content which the reader recognizes as grotesque, and at least an implicit moral standard, the latter being essential in a militant attitude to experience" (224). Hereafter cited in text.

6. Claudette Combes, *Paris dans* Les Misérables (Nantes: CID Editions, 1981), 33–37, provides a detailed map of the quarter, while likewise noting its infernal appearance. See also 186, regarding the modernized sewer.

7. For the representations of emperor and empire in *Châtiments*, see Jean Gaudon, *Le Temps de la Contemplation* (Paris: Flammarion, 1969), 161 and 167, and Ubersfeld, *Paroles*, 49.

8. Hugo, *Oeuvres*, exploits similar themes in his satirical *Châtiments*. For example, in "Apothéose" ("Apotheosis"; 8:629), "One gets attached to power and one eats France. / That is how a swindler becomes a statesman." In "L'Expiation" ("Expiation"; 8:703), Napoléon Bonaparte's excesses are punished by the "flashy Empire" of a mustachioed hoodlum. And in "L'égout de Rome" ("The Sewer of Rome"; 8:746), "rotten Caesars" end up in the cloaca with the garbage.

9. See Gohin, "Une histoire," 50. It is worth noting that Karl Marx took much the same tack in *The Eighteenth Brumaire of Louis Bonaparte* (1852), contemptuously measuring the nephew's coup d'état against the uncle's seizure of power from the Directory (the government of the First Republic from 1795 to 1799).

10. Thus, in "Nox" ("Night"), the opening poem of the collection, Hugo calls the middle class "vile herd, vile ooze" (*Oeuvres*, 8:574), its group mentality having reduced one and all to a kind of slimy sediment—like that found in the sewers.

Chapter 7. Dramatic Conventions

1. The technical term for multiple personalities is *personae*. Actually, Hugo "stages" Madeleine's psychic split in "A Tempest Within a Brain" (I.vii.3) as if it were occurring at once internally and externally.

2. According to Brombert, *Victor Hugo*, 108, the battle thus "marks the historical articulation in a providential drama which begins with the French Revolution and which, despite apparent setbacks, is not to be arrested."

3. Peter Brooks, *The Melodramatic Imagination: Balzac, Henry James, Melodrama, and the Mode of Excess* (New Haven: Yale University Press, 1976); hereafter cited in text. In *Early Novels*, I show the impact of melodra-

ma on the novels of Hugo's youth, including *The Last Day of a Condemned Man* and *The Hunchback of Notre Dame*.

4. Nor is Hugo's Rabelaisian delight in wordplay—the names for books, chapters, places, characters; the "graveyard humor" of the cemetery scene; the witty inventiveness of Gavroche or the verbal inebriation of Grantaire—peripheral to his concerns. When Jean Valjean abandons his position in Montreuil-sur-mer to replace Fantine as Cosette's parent, for example, the pun on *maire* = *mer* = *mère* (mayor, sea, mother) encapsulates his spiritual journey from paternalistic provider for the town, through a plunge off the galley ship, to the nurturing of a single child.

5. Readers familiar with Balzac's *Le Père Goriot* (1835; *Old Goriot*), the prototype for Christ-like paternal sacrifice, may see Thénardier as "competing" here with that other archvillain, Vautrin, who dreamed of becoming a slave owner in the American South.

6. See Jacques Seebacher, "La Mort de Jean Valjean," *Centenaire des Misérables 1862–1962: Hommage à Victor Hugo* (Strasbourg: Bulletin de la Faculté des Lettres de Strasbourg, 1962), 69–83. Similarly, the deaths by self-annihilation at the end of Hugo's later novels, *Toilers of the Sea* (1866), *The Man Who Laughs* (1869), and *Ninety-Three* (1874), can be viewed as leading, beyond tragedy, to transfiguration, knowledge, utopia.

Chapter 8. Vision, Lyricism, Poetry

1. The indissoluble relation for Hugo between the sublime and grotesque dates back to the *Preface to Cromwell* (1827). In *The Hunchback of Notre Dame* (1831), it is represented through the Gothic cathedral itself, as well as through the twinning of the hideous hunchback with the beautiful Gypsy dancer. See my treatment of these affiliations in *Early Novels*, 171–77, 186–93, and 199–206.

2. Victor Hugo, Preface to *Les Contemplations*, in *Oeuvres*, 9:60. See also Pierre Albouy, "Hugo, ou le Je éclaté," *Romantisme* 1–2 (1971): 58.

3. For an analysis of the relationship between Javert's character and Jean Valjean's, see especially Piroué, *VH romancier*, 63–67; Jean-Pierre Richard, "Petite lecture de Javert," *Revue des sciences humaines* 156 (October–December 1974): 597–607; Kathryn M. Grossman, "Hugo's Romantic Sublime: Beyond Chaos and Convention in *Les Misérables*," *Philological Quarterly* 60, no. 4 (Fall 1981): 471–86; and Jacques Dubois, "L'Affreux Javert: *The champ you love to hate*," *Hugo dans les marges*, eds. Lucien Dällenbach and Laurent Jenny (Geneva: Zoe, 1985), 9–34.

4. See, for instance, Gaudon, *Temps*, 468.

5. It is tempting to see in Hugo's masterful expression of many voices—epic, dramatic, satiric, lyrical, visionary—the domination by creative genius of a hereditary predisposition to what was, most likely, schizophrenia.

6. See Gohin, "Une histoire," 31, 34, 40–41.

7. Thus, for Brombert, *Victor Hugo*, 104, "the discovery of the heroic father [Colonel Pontmercy] is bound up with the discovery of history as progress."

8. In particular, Enjolras echoes the ideas of Pierre Leroux, the "utopian socialist" thinker who had a profound influence on the entire generation of romantic writers, including Hugo and George Sand. In works such as *De l'Egalité* (1838; *On Equality*) and *De l'humanité* (1840; *On Humanity*), Leroux defined his vision of the ideal future through the concepts of "humanity" (what links each individual to past, present, and future generations), "solidarity" (the equivalent of Christian charity, that is, of love for one's fellow human beings), and "perfectibility" (the possibility of moral and social progress).

9. See Jay Clayton, *Romantic Vision and the Novel* (Cambridge: Harvard University Press, 1984), 7: "Transcendence expands the self, giving the poet access to a new being."

10. Guy Rosa, "Jean Valjean (1, 2, 6): Réalisme et irréalisme des *Misérables*," *Lire* Les Misérables, 205–38, applies the notion of *irrealism* to Hugo's transgression of realist conventions in the novel. See also Pierre Albouy, *La Création mythologique chez Victor Hugo* (Paris: José Corti, 1963), 156, 157, and 497. Regarding Jean Valjean's representation of the visionary poet, see Brombert, *Victor Hugo*, 134.

Selected Bibliography

Primary Works

Oeuvres complètes. Edited by Jean Massin. 18 volumes. Paris: Le Club Français du Livre, 1967–70. See especially *Les Misérables*, volume 11, 1969. Superb critical apparatus, including historical background and detailed chronology. Available in major research libraries.

Oeuvres complètes. Edited by the Groupe Inter-universitaire de Travail sur Victor Hugo. 15 volumes. Paris: Editions Robert Laffont, 1985. See especially *Les Misérables*, volume "Roman 2," edited by Guy and Annette Rosa. Contains an introduction, notes, and chronology of composition intended for nonspecialists.

Les Misérables. Edited by Guy Rosa and Nicole Savy. 3 volumes. Paris: Livre de Poche, 1985. Excellent introduction and critical notes aimed at the general public.

Les Misérables. Translated by Norman Denny. Harmondsworth: Penguin Books, 1980. Carries much of the beauty and force of Hugo's language but abridges some interesting longer passages.

Les Misérables. Translated by Lee Fahnestock and Norman MacAfee, based on the classic Charles E. Wilbour translation. Signet Classic. New York: New American Library, 1987. Very accurate, literal, complete rendition that does not quite capture the poetic power of the original.

Secondary Works

Books and Collections

Albouy, Pierre. *La Création mythologique chez Victor Hugo.* Paris: José Corti, 1963. Key study of the mythological aspects of Hugo's poetry, drama, and fiction.

Baudouin, Charles. *Psychanalyse de Victor Hugo.* 1943. Paris: Armand Colin, 1972. Freudian interpretation of recurring images and themes in Hugo.

Bowman, Frank Paul. *French Romanticism: Intertextual and Interdisciplinary Readings.* Baltimore: Johns Hopkins University Press, 1990. Places the French romantic movement within its cultural, political, religious, philosophical, and historical context.

Brochu, André. *Hugo, Amour/Crime/Révolution: Essai sur* Les Misérables. Montréal: Presses de l'Université de Montréal, 1974. Investigates the repeating themes and plot patterns in the novel, highlighting the interactions between the major characters.

Brombert, Victor. *The Romantic Prison: The French Tradition.* Princeton: Princeton University Press, 1978. Excellent chapter on Hugo situates the variations on the prison motif in *Les Misérables* in relation to his other works, as well as to such writers as Pascal, Stendhal, Nerval, Baudelaire, and Sartre.

————. *Victor Hugo and the Visionary Novel.* Cambridge: Harvard University Press, 1984. Of interest to specialists and nonspecialists alike, a penetrating analysis of Hugo's fiction that centers on its epic, historical, mythical, and visionary dimensions. Highly useful chapter on *Les Misérables.*

Brooks, Peter. *The Melodramatic Imagination: Balzac, Henry James, Melodrama, and the Mode of Excess.* New Haven: Yale University Press, 1976. Explores the fundamental elements of melodrama, an extremely popular post-Revolutionary genre, and illustrates their incorporation by romantic and realist writers, including Hugo.

Centenaire des Misérables, *1862–1962: Hommage à Victor Hugo.* Strasbourg: Bulletin de la Faculté des Lettres de Strasbourg, 1962. Contains 15 essays, many still important, on various aspects of *Les Misérables.*

Combes, Claudette. *Paris dans* Les Misérables. Nantes: CID Editions, 1981. Comprehensive examination of the topology, image, and role of Paris in the novel, supported by numerous maps and photographs.

Europe. Special issue (in French) on *Les Misérables.* 40.394–95 (February–March 1962). Twelve essays devoted to the text, with several character studies and a summary of the film versions.

Selected Bibliography

Gaudon, Jean. *Le Temps de la Contemplation*. Paris: Flammarion, 1969. Magisterial study of Hugo's poetic universe, with particular emphasis on the poetry and fiction of the 1840s and 1850s. Invaluable for understanding the genesis of *Les Misérables* (as *Les Misères*) in 1846 and its relation to the great poetic works of the period.

Grant, Richard B. *The Perilous Quest: Image, Myth, and Prophecy in the Narratives of Victor Hugo*. Durham: Duke University Press, 1968. Investigates the heroic quest myth in Hugo's novels, drama, and epic poetry. Connects the satanic and redemptive imagery associated with Jean Valjean to the poetry of the 1850s and the earlier fiction.

Grossman, Kathryn M. *Figuring Transcendence in* Les Misérables: *Hugo's Romantic Sublime*. Carbondale: Southern Illinois University Press, 1994. Examines recurrent motifs in both the story line and the digressions of *Les Misérables* in light of other Hugo works and recent studies of metaphor and the romantic sublime

Hugo: Les Misérables. *Actes du colloque du 19 novembre 1994 à la Sorbonne.* Edited by Pierre Brunel. Paris: Editions InterUniversitaires, 1994. Current scholarship, focusing on Parts 1 and 2 of *Les Misérables*, intended for nonspecialists

Journet, René, and Guy Robert. *Le Mythe du peuple dans* Les Misérables. Paris: Editions Sociales, 1964. Considers the people of Paris in the novel as representing the efforts of the nation to realize the goals of the French Revolution

Laforgue, Pierre. *Gavroche: Étude sur* Les Misérables. Paris: SEDES, 1994. Explores Hugo's ideology of misery through the character of Gavroche, symbol of political anarchy and a unifying element of the text.

Laster, Arnaud. *Pleins Feux sur Victor Hugo*. Paris: Comédie-Française, 1981. Very useful, accessible overview of Hugo's life, works, characters, relationships, and literary fortunes, as well as of the musical, stage, film, radio, and television adaptations of his writings.

Lire Les Misérables. Edited by Anne Ubersfeld and Guy Rosa. Paris: José Corti, 1985. Excellent collection of essays on the novel, representing contemporary Hugo scholarship in France. Includes a bibliography.

Phalèse, Hubert de. *Dictionnaire des* Misérables. Collection Cap'Agreg 6. Paris: Nizet, 1994. Lexicon of proper names and terms of particular interest in *Les Misérables*, supplemented by a current bibliography.

Piroué, Georges. *Victor Hugo romancier ou les dessus de l'inconnu*. Paris: Denoël, 1964. Insightful meditations on the repeating patterns of character and theme in Hugo's prose fiction.

Savey-Casard, Paul. *Le Crime et la peine dans l'oeuvre de Victor Hugo*. Paris: Presses Universitaires de la France, 1956. Classic study of the evolution of Hugo's views on crime, punishment, poverty, and criminals.

Simaïka, Raouf. *L'Inspiration épique dans les romans de Victor Hugo.* Geneva: Droz, 1962. Explores the epic qualities of Hugo's novels and their relation to his lyricism. Chapter on *Les Misérables* establishes an important link between Jean Valjean and the French people's striving for progress.

Ubersfeld, Anne. *Paroles de Hugo.* Paris: Messidor, 1985. Studies romantic discourse in Hugo, especially its grotesque, utopian, and theatrical aspects, from a psychoanalytical viewpoint. Stimulating analysis of Jean Valjean's dream and of the role of names in *Les Misérables.*

Victor Hugo, Les Misérables: *"La preuve par les abîmes."* Actes du colloque du 2 décembre 1994 à l'Ecole Normale Supérieure. Edited by José-Luis Diaz. *Romantisme:* Colloques series. Volume 21. Paris: SEDES, 1994. Outstanding collection of studies by leading Hugo scholars aimed at nonspecialists.

Articles

Cudmore, Pierre-Etienne. "Jean Valjean et les avatars du poète éponyme." *French Review* 61, no. 2 (1987): 170–77. Argues that Jean Valjean is a figure of the creative poet, and so of Hugo himself.

Dubois, Jacques. "L'Affreux Javert: *The champ you love to hate.*" In *Hugo dans les marges.* Edited by Lucien Dällenbach and Laurent Jenny. Geneva: Zoe, 1985. Studies the relationship between Javert and Jean Valjean and their function as reverse images of each other.

Gaudon, Jean. "Digressions hugoliennes." In volume 14 of *Oeuvres complètes.* Edited by Jean Massin. Paris: Le Club Français du Livre, 1967–70. Discusses the integral role of Hugo's narrative digressions, including those on Waterloo, Paris, and the convent in *Les Misérables.*

Grimaud, Michel. "De Victor Hugo à Homère-Hogu: l'onomastique des *Misérables.*" *L'Esprit Créateur* 16 (Fall 1976): 220–30. Examines the role of characters' names in the novel.

La Carrera, Rosalina de. "History's Unconscious in Victor Hugo's *Les Misérables.*" *Modern Language Notes* 96, no. 4 (May 1981): 839–55. Reads the novel as an allegory of Freudian psychoanalysis: the process of recovering repressed historical memories also reveals the discontinuities of progress.

Leuilliot, Bernard. "Présentation des *Misérables.*" In Volume 11 of *Oeuvres complètes.* Edited by Jean Massin. Paris: Le Club Français du Livre, 1967–70. The circumstances surrounding the composition of the novel, its chronology, structure, and poetic qualities.

Mauron, Charles. "Les Personnages de Victor Hugo: Étude Psychocritique." In Volume 2 of *Oeuvres complètes.* Edited by Jean Massin. Paris: Le Club Français du Livre, 1967–70. Psychoanalytical reading of the relations between Hugo's characters in both the drama and fiction.

Selected Bibliography

Maxwell, Richard. "Mystery and Revelation in *Les Misérables.*" *Romanic Review* 73, no. 3 (1982):314–30. Studies the mysteries of crime and misery, as exemplified by Thénardier and Jean Valjean, in light of Eugène Sue's *Mystères de Paris* and Michelet's *Le Peuple.*

Meschonnic, Henri. "La Poésie dans *Les Misérables.*" In Volume 11 of *Oeuvres complètes.* Edited by Jean Massin. Paris: Le Club Français du Livre, 1967–70. Examines the poetic vocabulary, rhythm, and symbolism in *Les Misérables.*

Ricatte, Robert. "*Les Misérables*: Hugo et ses personnages." In Volume 11 of *Oeuvres complètes.* Edited by Jean Massin. Paris: Le Club Français du Livre, 1967–70. The psychology of Hugo's characters as revealed through his use of language.

Richard, Jean-Pierre. "Petite lecture de Javert." *Revue des sciences humaines* 156 (October–December 1974): 597-607. Discusses Javert's function as Jean Valjean's dark and legal double, as well as the material and spatial imagery associated with his character.

Savy, Nicole. "Un roman de geste: *Les Misérables.*" In *Hugo le fabuleux.* Actes du Colloque de Cerisy. 30 June–10 July, 1985. Edited by Jacques Seebacher and Anne Ubersfeld. Paris: Seghers, 1985. 108–15. Considers *Les Misérables* to be exemplary of what Erich Auerbach defines as "figurative realism."

———. "Victor Hugo féministe?" *La Pensée* 245 (May–June 1985): 7–17. Important study of the apparent contradiction between Hugo's political feminism and his traditional characterizations of women.

Seebacher, Jacques. "Poétique et politique de la paternité chez Victor Hugo." In Volume 12 of *Oeuvres complètes.* Edited by Jean Massin. Paris: Le Club Français du Livre, 1967–70. Demonstrates the close affiliation for Hugo of spiritual progress, democratic politics, and poetic endeavor in *Les Misérables* and in the poetry of the 1850s and 1860s.

———. "Misères de la coupure, coupure des *Misérables.*" *Revue des sciences humaines* 156 (October–December 1974): 569–80. Argues that the 13-year break in the composition of the text, which allowed Hugo to reorganize it around Part 4, can be attributed as much to inner conflicts regarding his deceased daughter Léopoldine as to political events.

Turton, Derek. "Thematic Imagery in Hugo's *Les Misérables.*" *Revue de l'Université d'Ottawa* 42, no. 4 (October–December 1972): 550–69. Correlation between the themes of moral regeneration and political progress in *Les Misérables.*

Vernier, France. "*Les Misérables*: ce livre est dangereux." *L'Arc* 57 (1974): 33-39. Claims that the revolutionary aspects of the text help to account not only for its popular success but for the establishment of the insurrectional Commune in 1871.

————. "*Les Misérables* ou: De la modernité." In *Hugo le fabuleux*. Actes du Colloque de Cerisy. 30 June–10 July, 1985. Edited by Jacques Seebacher and Anne Ubersfeld. Paris: Seghers, 1985. Discusses the ways in which the novel can be viewed as both typically and atypically modernist.

Welsh, Alexander. "Opening and Closing *Les Misérables*." *Nineteenth-Century Fiction* 33, no. 11 (1978): 8–23. Analyzes the contrasting fates of the two heroes of Hugo's historical novel from the standpoint of nineteenth-century views of history.

Biographies of Hugo

Decaux, Alain. *Victor Hugo*. Paris: Perrin, 1984. Richly detailed account of Hugo's life, with brief quotations from his literary works, political writings, and personal correspondence.

Maurois, André. *Victor Hugo*. Translated from the French *Olympio: La Vie de Victor Hugo* by Gerard Hopkins. London: Jonathan Cape, 1956. Lively, well-documented biography.

Bibliographies

Grant, Elliott M. *Victor Hugo: A Select and Critical Bibliography*. Chapel Hill: University of North Carolina, 1967.

Ward, Patricia. *Carnet bibliographique Victor Hugo: Oeuvres et critique 1978–1980*. Paris: Lettres modernes, 1985.

————, and Bernadette Lintz-Murphy. "Carnet bibliographique Victor Hugo: Oeuvres et critique 1981–1983." *Revue des Lettres Modernes* (1992): 1096–99.

Index

Index

141

Index

The Author

Kathryn M. Grossman received her doctorate in Romance languages at Yale University. She is currently professor of French at Penn State University, where she has also served as an associate director in the International Programs office and as head of the French department. She is the author of two books, *The Early Novels of Victor Hugo: Towards a Poetics of Harmony* (1986) and *Figuring Transcendence in* Les Misérables: *Hugo's Romantic Sublime* (1994), as well as of numerous articles on politically engaged writers such as Hugo, Dickens, Sand, Orwell, and Zamiatin. She is at present completing a book on Hugo's later novels.